BUD

A Parable of God's Sovereignty

By **Dr. Cynthia Perkins**

WESTBOW
PRESS®
A DIVISION OF THOMAS NELSON
& ZONDERVAN

WestBow Press books may be ordered through booksellers or by contacting:

WestBow Press
A Division of Thomas Nelson & Zondervan
1663 Liberty Drive
Bloomington, IN 47403
www.westbowpress.com
844-714-3454

Because of the dynamic nature of the Internet, any web addresses or links contained in this book may have changed since publication and may no longer be valid. The views expressed in this work are solely those of the author and do not necessarily reflect the views of the publisher, and the publisher hereby disclaims any responsibility for them.

Any people depicted in stock imagery provided by Getty Images are models, and such images are being used for illustrative purposes only.
Certain stock imagery © Getty Images.

Interior Image Credit: Juanita June Grugan-White

Scripture marked (NKJV) taken from the New King James Version®. Copyright © 1982 by Thomas Nelson. Used by permission. All rights reserved.

Scripture quotations marked (ESV) are from the ESV® Bible (The Holy Bible, English Standard Version®), copyright © 2001 by Crossway, a publishing ministry of Good News Publishers. Used by permission. All rights reserved.

Scripture marked (NASB) taken from the New American Standard Bible (NASB) Copyright ©1960, 1962, 1963, 1968, 1971, 1972, 1973, 1975, 1977, 1995 by The Lockman Foundation, La Habra, CA. All rights reserved. Used by Permission. www.lockman.org.

Scripture quotations marked (NIV) are taken from the Holy Bible, New International Version®, NIV®. Copyright © 1973, 1978, 1984, 2011 by Biblica, Inc.® Used by permission of Zondervan. All rights reserved worldwide. www.zondervan.com The "NIV" and "New International Version" are trademarks registered in the United States Patent and Trademark Office by Biblica, Inc.®

ISBN: 978-1-6642-2325-7 (sc)
ISBN: 978-1-6642-2324-0 (hc)
ISBN: 978-1-6642-2349-3 (e)

Library of Congress Control Number: 2021902787

Print information available on the last page.

WestBow Press rev. date: 03/31/2021

ENDORSEMENTS

This book tells the Life story of one of "the least of these" that Jesus spoke of in Matthew 25:40. In telling the story of Bud, Dr. Perkins shows how even the least among us can be used by God if we respond with simple faith. Bud left a mark on everyone he met, and everyone was remembered by him. Bud's life always mattered and this book reveals how God used Bud in His master plan.

Bob Chatham (who lived part of the story).

Bud was likely the most repulsive person I ever met as a boy. There was absolutely nothing about the man that would attract a stranger to strike up a relationship but you'll finish this book wanting to become more like him. Page by page, the honest exposition Dr. Perkins provides, will open your eyes and your heart."

Michael Cate, former history instructor University of Arkansas Rich Mountain, author and publisher.

DEDICATION

BUD - A Parable of the Sovereignty of God is dedicated to God's sovereignty. He sent Bud, a man with the mind of a child and the Spirit's heart, to Earth to be a servant and a witness. God said, "I have plans for you…Bud!"

In some ways, Bud bore a resemblance to God's Son. He was a shepherd who loved the church like a husband loves his wife showing grace and love beyond what mere human beings could understand.

How marvelous it is to know our God is in control. His kingdom is come. His will is good and perfect on Earth, as it is in Heaven.

THANK YOUS

To the following I give honor and praise to God for providing help with this project:

The Donica family (my biological family), Riley, Jane, Sherry, Robin, and David, embracing Bud as a part of our family. Always helping him and seeing to his needs. Never being critical. We loved him as our kin.

The Perkins family (my husband and children), Kent, Ann Marie and Keri Lynn. Love for Bud continued with us, the extended family. Helping him with his animals, church activities, food, etc., and always making sure he was ok.

Coy Fairless from Brushy Ridge, who had a heart for Bud, and always had him come for the Fairless family reunions, birthdays and celebrations. He always said Bud's handshake made him feel special.

Marie Phillips, Faith Lynch, Bob Chattham and Kent Perkins, who without pay or credit edited BUD and gave me confidence to continue working to complete the task.

Johnny Edwards who was Bud's caregiver until his trip Home.

Tammy Cady, a wonderful friend and sister in Christ. She is the project designer for this book. God definitely sent her to me at this specific time. Her gift of technology, artistry, creativity, musicianship and her commitment to helping others proves her love for Jesus, and Jesus' love for her. She is also very patient and kind personally to me. Thank you, Tammy.

A huge "thank you" to those missionaries of the Kiamichi Mountains, who established area churches, and, because of their efforts, those like Bud had the opportunity to accept the gospel and have a church family. With the churches' help, Bud grew both physically and spiritually. I was an eye-witness of his growth.

ACKNOWLEDGEMENTS

I will start by acknowledging the foremost persons who helped with this project, the Trinity. They wrote; *"Unless you become as a little child you cannot enter the kingdom of heaven." (Matthew 19:14 - paraphrased from NKJV).* Then they created Bud to prove their point! The most important thanks goes to God, my Father, who made Bud's life such a testimony that no one can deny His grace and love. His sovereignty is beyond measure. Bud proclaimed the glory of the Lord each and every day of his life. Thank you Father. May you have all the glory, honor and praise.

Ada Chatham, who helped Bud with his goats, and was such a help in my desire to write **BUD**. I lived with Ada for a period of six months, and during my stay I witnessed Bud's daily care of his herd. He cared for them like family. Ada was an exceptional cook. Her kindness toward Bud included sharing her meals.

Thank you to Zafra Church. You gave Bud a home, a place of fellowship and family. You were his sisters and brothers in Christ.

 Illustrator: Juanita June Grugan-White taught art in both public and private schools, and colleges for twenty-eight years. She received her BA and MA degrees from Southeastern Oklahoma State University. She was the recipient of the Minnie M. Baker Art Award, and the National Endowment of the Arts and Humanities Scholarship. Mrs. Grugan-White lives in Marietta, Oklahoma. **BUD** is her first book to illustrate.

FOREWORD

Bud lived in the community of Zafra named in the book.

It's hard to believe Bud's life was actually true, because it was more like a fairy tale… "denoting something regarded as resembling a story in being magical, idealized or extremely happy." Bud's story is the same concept; however, it's TRUE! It's magical in the sense that Bud believed God, and in believing, His power and glory was always at Bud's request.

Most fairy tales end with… "and they lived happily ever after." Bud did.

God's sovereignty oozed out of Bud. His Son told us not to worry about what we should eat, drink, wear, etc. God said He knows what we need before we ask. He leads us in the paths of righteousness. He promises His goodness and mercy will follow us all the days of our lives!

NOTE:

BUD is based on a true story. The names and places are frequently altered or changed to enhance the story.

CONTENTS

PREFACE

BUD

"Your eyes saw my unformed substance;
in your book were written every one of them,
the days that were formed for me,
when as yet there was none of them."
~ Psalm 139:16 (ESV) ~

As a child, Bud seemed scary to me. To a four-year-old, the very tall, black-haired, wide-eyed man with a misshaped face and huge mole protruding out on his right cheek caused me to shudder and slither safely behind my daddy's leg.

Bud had a wide smile showing dirty, yellow teeth and red raw gums. Adding the bad smell, that I later found out was "goat," made me wonder if this was a man or a monster!

Bud always walked up, too close, to the person he was about to speak with, invading their space. But before he got to his destination, the smell of wood smoke blended with goat made "rank" an understatement.

Bud's unusual dress of several layers, plus food stains from days of wearing the same clothes, added to his creepy demeanor.

When Bud opened his mouth to speak, out came stutter and spit. The spit would reach your face. The stutter would begin with your name; "Aa---ba---den". The end of his word or sort of sentences would always end with "den." As he spoke, his hand automatically reached out for a hand shake. Bud's hand shake shook the receiver's entire body.

Suddenly, it became clear there was no "scary" in Bud. His eyes lit up with kindness. Like sun coming out from behind a cloud. Bud's great big ear-to-ear grin spread warmth to the receivers.

Bud was real and simple. No matter the reactions of others, whether kind or mean, ugly or beautiful, Bud stayed...well...Bud.

Mostly Bud's simplicity guided him to his greatest loves of all: God his Father; Jesus his Brother; and the Spirit who was his guide.

Talk about special! Bud was special, in the best definition of the word...

> ~ Exceptionally Distinct
>> ~ Memorable
>>> ~ Remarkable!

A megaphone of God's sovereignty...BUD:

> Just one person, alone, in the body of a man with the mind of a five-year-old, speech impaired, penniless, unschooled...none of it mattered, because **Bud belonged to God!**

CHAPTER ONE

- LOST -

Once he was lost and has been found.
~ Luke 15:32 (NASB) ~

Darkness had started covering the thick wooded mountains. A five-year-old boy was lost somewhere. He had been missing for three days. The community of Zafra was on the hunt. His name, Ward Wilson; nicknamed---Bud. Searchers walked, while some road horseback. An unspoken realization wrenched their minds. If Bud was not found alive today, he would probably be found dead!

Three days before, the temperature was 65 degrees. It had dropped 30 degrees lower with strong winds. Not unusual for these mountains.

Just about dark, a man in the hunt, Preston, yelled, "There he is!" Bud was lying down. Hearing the approaching search party, he was completely terrified and began to run.

Preston yelled, "Rope 'em or he'll get away!" The rope flew over him tightening around his chest. He screamed horrifying sounds. He clawed and scratched at the rope and the men trying to rescue him.

"Maybe we can show him there ain't nothin' to be afraid of," Preston exclaimed.

Bud was trying to speak, but only shuttering groans and sounds of pure terror came out of his mouth.

Pastor Dalton hurried over with a blanket. "Here, wrap 'em up in this. He's wet, cold and covered in mud."

"Completely cover 'em up before he hurts himself or someone else!" Preston instructed.

1

The blanket suddenly covered his face and caused him to pass out.

"He's fine." Preston assured everyone. "With him out, it'll be easier to get 'em home."

After he was wrapped up, Preston mounted his horse, and Pastor Dalton laid Bud in his arms. Preston held Bud tightly. He knew he was exhausted, malnourished and dehydrated. Sleeping would help.

As they headed to the Wilson's farm, Pastor Dalton gave a praise. "Only by the grace of the Lord have we found 'em. He should be dead after three days alone in these here woods. It's a wonder he weren't snake bit or worse. He coulda been attacked by a varmint! These here mountains are full of 'em."

Everyone shook their heads in agreement. It wasn't often a person witnessed a miracle, but the hunting party just had.

***

Mama and Papa Wilson were out on the porch waiting for news from the searchers. As they rode up, Mama Wilson saw Preston holding a bundle in his arms. She cried, "BUD!"

Preston smiled, "We found 'em."

Pastor Dalton took Bud. He was still out cold. "Mrs. Wilson, let's get him inside before we take 'em outta the blanket. When we found 'em, he was scared of us."

Both Mama and Papa Wilson were crying with joy to see Bud. They thought he was dead.

As soon as Preston begin to open the blanket, Bud woke up. At first, he was terrified. Seeing the terror in his eyes, Mama Wilson reached out calling to him, "Bud, it's Mama!"

He ran to the corner, laid down, and curled into a fetal position making whimpering noises.

"He's been lost too long. It'll take a few days fer 'em to regain his complete memory Mrs. Wilson, so please don't worry. He'll be ok after he gets food and rest. He'll settle down," Preston reassured her.

Pastor Dalton, with hat in hand, humbly asked, "Could we pray?"

Too emotional to speak, Mr. Wilson nodded his head "yes."

Looking up the pastor prayed, "Father, thank yah fer 'llowin' us to find Bud. We knowed he is truly yours, 'cause you led us to 'em. He's alive! Truly this miracle belongs to you. You're the protector of Bud's life. May Bud always be yours. In Jesus' name, Amen."

Everyone repeated "Amen."

***

At this time, most who helped find Bud didn't understand how he was the Father's. But Pastor Dalton did. God's sovereignty surrounded Bud. It was as if God said to him, *"I kill and I make alive; I wound and I heal; and there is none that can deliver out of my hand." (Deuteronomy 32:39 - ESV)*

CHAPTER TWO

- FAVOR WITH GOD AND MAN -
He grew in wisdom and stature...
~ Luke 2:52 (NIV) ~

After Bud's terrifying ordeal, his mind remained at the age of five. He was stuck in a mental time warp. His speech never developed. He spoke noises, rather than words.

Words he tried to speak were pronounced with a hard stutter. Words were put together in strange ways; very few and hard to understand. Most of his conversation was just a repeat of what someone had just said to him. His words came out in mostly letter sounds, and they always ended with "den."

He grew physically like anyone else, but the five-year-old child in his heart and mind stayed stuck!

***

Mr. and Mrs. Wilson kept Bud at home except for church. The church became his social connection. Every time the doors were open, Bud was there.

"Good mornin' Bud," Pastor Dalton stuck his hand into Bud's. A hard shake followed.

"Pass---ter---Dah---ll---ten—den," Bud answered. He smiled his ear-to-ear grin, continuing around the church porch, shaking hands and pronouncing everyone's name. He had to finish his ritual before he sat down.

Bud, Mama and Papa Wilson always sat in the same spot. If a visitor happened to sit there, Bud would push them over, so the family could sit down. The visitor didn't understand Bud's intrusion, so the church ladies would rush to intervene and explain the situation.

Thelma Lou, a friendly outgoing talker asked, "Bud, did yah bring you'rn Bible today? Don't you young'uns ferget you're in my class this mornin."

Daisy handed Mrs. Wilson sacks of fresh corn. Bertha gave her two dozen eggs.

"I hope you'll like these here eggs, Mrs. Wilson. My hens 're layin' up a storm. I thought your family could use 'um. I'm sho'nuff Bud can eat his weight in eggs." She gave a gentle chuckle.

"Same here," sweet Daisy chimed in. She was always happy with a lively laugh that made her tummy bounce. "Our corn crop is a blessin' this year, so's we're sharin' it. We know how Bud loves to eat!"

Mama Wilson gratefully accepted. "Thank y'all. We sho' can use these here goodies."

Ethel, Pastor Dalton's wife, begin playing the piano announcing it was time to begin the service.

Bud loved singing. He always sang at the top of his lungs. He couldn't pronounce the words, so he just pronounced "at" them. What words he didn't know, he made up:

> Ben---I---seez da blud. *(When I see the blood.)*
> Ben---I---seez da blud. *(When I see the blood.)*
> Ben---I---seez da blud. *(When I see the blood.)*
> Izs---vel---pas---oh---ver---ooo. *(I will pass over you.)*

Rocking back and forth out of rhythm, off pitch and loud made his singing a noise of joy!

Bud's enthusiastic singing helped the entire congregation lift their voices in praise to God. The congregation might not have caught on to Bud's leadership, but Pastor Dalton and Sister Ethel surely did.

***

As Bud got older, Mama and Papa Wilson knew he should attend school. With his mind stuck at age five and his limited speech, would they accept him?

Mama and Papa Wilson talked to Pastor Dalton. "It won't hurt fer you tuh try. Bud is a good boy. He isn't afraid to join in. Havin' other children 'round 'em will help 'em learn to communicate and possibly speak. If he only learns tuh get along with others, its an important enough reason fer him tuh go tuh school. Learnin' to read is essential to understandin' things. He needs a chance. Specially, it's important to be able to read the Word of God."

The Wilsons took the pastor's advice. The timing was perfect. Bud had just turned seven. They prayed that if nothing else, he would learn to speak where he could be understood and to get along with others.

CHAPTER THREE

- EDUCATION -

So the Lord said to him,
"Who has made man's mouth?
Or who makes him mute, the deaf, the seeing, or
the blind? Have not I, the Lord?"
~ Exodus 4:11 (NKJV) ~

Zafra School consisted of first through eighth grade. The teachers, Mr. and Mrs. Elder, were two of the finest. They were kind and poised, setting godly examples for their students.

Every day Mr. and Mrs. Elder dressed professionally. Mr. Elder usually came wearing a unique tie, which caught the student's attention. The girls watched as Mrs. Elder would "freshen up" by combing her hair, powdering her face and putting on lipstick.

***

Mrs. Elder taught first through fourth in the "little room." Mr. Elder taught fifth through eighth in the "big room." First through eighth grade consisted of about 40 students.

***

Every day after the first bell, all students would gather in the "big room" for the morning ceremony, which consisted of singing folk songs, saluting the flag, praying the Lord's prayer and reading from the Bible.

The "drinking fountain" was a bucket of water with a dipper. Everyone drank from the same dipper with no thoughts about germs.

The gymnasium was an outdoor gravel basketball court. The court leaned downhill on one side causing everyone to slide to a stop. Students practiced in their bare feet until November when everyone received a pair of new or slightly used shoes for the winter ball season.

The class rooms were kept clean and beautifully decorated. Each room catered to the student's ages. Every student had their own wooden desk, with a huge cubby hole at the bottom for books and school work. A coat closet where student's names were written above the hooks was behind a large wall panel.

The coat closet doubled for the library. Mrs. Elder was librarian for each room. They were filled with exciting books of mystery, heroes, animals, Bible stories and history.

Students who read the most books per week received candy corn as a special treat. Store-bought candy wasn't readily available in these mountains. Everyone worked hard at reading to win the candy.

Each day, Mrs. Elder read from a book. She made the story come alive. The students got lost in their imaginations of the character's lives.

***

The school's toilets were outside; no indoor plumbing. To get permission to use the toilets, students raised their hand: one finger up for a quicker toilet time; two fingers up for a longer toilet time.

***

Each room was warmed by a big wood stove. Student's sitting farthest away took trips over to the stove to warm up. The high ceiling would not allow for a warm room.

***

Lunch time was called "dinner." Kids would line up and march to stand behind their seats. Then, Mr. and Mrs. Elder lead the students in prayer:

God is great.
God is good.
Let us thank Him
For our food.
Amen

Every day delicious, made-from-scratch food was served. Most everyone cleaned their plate. "NO TALKING" was allowed during lunch. If caught, punishment was a ten-minute timeout of recess. Nobody talked!

***

Every year the school had a Christmas program. The biggest tree the men of the community could find was placed in the middle of the room. The huge doors, dividing the big and little room, were completely opened to make an area for the giant cedar.

All the grades joined in making tree decorations. Strands of popcorn, cranberries and colored-paper chains draped its branches. Painted pine cones and glittered holly hung on the tree. Lots of lights and icicles made it something to behold.

Every student performed Christmas carols and recited Christmas poetry. The "big room" performed a Christmas play, while the "little room" presented "The Nativity."

Every Christmas Mr. and Mrs. Elder brought a gift for every child. Gifts for girls were for their "hope chest;" gifts for boys were for hunting or sports. Christmas was a very special time for the school and the community.

This was the environment where Bud received his one and only year of formal education.

***

Waking Bud early, Mama Wilson yelled, "Bud, it's pert-near time tuh go tuh school."

"Sch---oo---ll---den," he answered as he jumped out of bed.

"Yes, I want you learnin', readin' and writin'. They may not allow yuh to go, but we're a goanna try."

"O---k-k-k---den." Bud was excited to get to play with other kids.

Mrs. Wilson was apprehensive. "Papa, I sho' hope Bud is able tuh attend school. He can't speak very well. I ain't sho' they'll take 'em."

"Don't worry mama," papa chided. "He'll learn how to speak bein' 'round all those kids ever' day. He'll learn to at least make sentences. It'll be good fer 'em."

Still unsure, she looked at papa. "I sho' hope y'ur right dad. Bein' turned down is hard to swaller."

"Come on Bud. We'd better get ta' goin'." Bud came into the room, his flour sack in hand, filled with a bit of paper and a pencil, grinning ear-to-ear, ready to go!

***

The walk to school helped calm Mama Wilson's nerves. As she got closer though, her fears kicked in. She thought, "What if Bud is turned down? Bud is my special child and it's hard tuh see 'em hurt. She looked up praying, 'Oh God, help us.'" That was all she needed to say.

***

Mr. and Mrs. Elder stood on the school porch as Bud and Mrs. Wilson walked down the driveway. All the students were at morning recess. They had heard about Bud starting school. Most stopped their playing and stared, whispering to each other about Bud coming to school.

For Mama Wilson, the walk to the porch seemed long. The teachers were smiling, patiently waiting.

Mrs. Wilson introduced herself. "Good mornin'. I'm Mrs. Wilson. This here's my son Ward. We call 'em Bud."

"Good day Mrs. Wilson. I'm Mr. Elder. This is my wife Mrs. Elder. She will be teaching Bud."

Mr. and Mrs. Elder reached out and shook Bud's hand. "Me---sss—ter---Ell---der---den." He shook hard. Then he switched, shaking Mrs. Elder's hand. "Mm—sss---Ell---der---den." As he shook their hands, he kept smiling his big ear-to-ear grin. They couldn't help joining in with Bud's smile.

"Please come in and we'll visit about Bud starting school." Mrs. Elder led the way to Mr. Elder's room and asked, "Bud, would you like to go play with the students while we visit with your mother about your attending school?"

"Pa---ll---aaa---den," Bud repeated.

Mr. Elder walked to the door and called for one of the older students. "Liz, come here please." Liz came running. She knew Bud from church and hoped he would be allowed to attend school. "Liz, please take Bud out to play and introduce him to the other students."

Liz grabbed Bud's hand. "Glad to Mr. Elder. Come on Bud, let's go swing." Bud didn't hesitate with Liz pulling him out the door.

12

Mrs. Wilson looked a little squeamish as Bud ran out to play. His only contact with other children was at church; a much smaller group of kids who had grown to accept Bud.

But this was a much bigger group of students, some twice Bud's age and twice his size. She feared he would be misunderstood and made fun of because of his speech and kind spirit.

Mr. Elder spotted the questioning look on Mama Wilson's face. "Don't worry Mrs. Wilson. We have many fine students who will help take care of Bud and will tell us if there are any problems."

Mama Wilson sat down slowly as she looked around at the inspiring room. Mr. Elder sat at his desk. "We have heard about Bud and will gladly teach him all we can. Please explain to us his situation. We want to hear everything from you."

Mrs. Wilson's eyes moistened, as she began to speak. "About two years ago, Bud got lost fer three days. On the third day, he was found. He was suh scared he tried tuh run. So's to catch 'em, they had to rope 'em. If he hadn't been found, he would uh died. His fear musta made his mind stop growin'. Since then, he's not been able to talk 'ceptin' with a stutter. He can't make words tuh make sentences. Mostly, he just repeats what someone says to 'em." She began to cry. Mrs. Elder patted her hand compassionately. "Mostly, he only says the name of those he's 'round. Fer some unknown reason he always puts 'den' on the end. We don't know why."

"He gives no trouble. Tuh the best of his ability, he will do what you'ns ask. He's gentle and kind tuh everyone, includin' animals. Oh, yes, and he never meets a stranger," added Mama Wilson.

Mrs. Elder smiled. "That's all you can ask from anyone, to do the best they can. We are glad you're willing to allow us to teach Bud. We don't have a lot of materials for this special challenge. That is to say, we are a very poor school district. However, we will use all the resources we have available to work with Bud. Our goal will be to teach him to read and write."

Mrs. Wilson's heart beat faster. She was excited for her son. "Thank ya'll." She smiled through her tears. "I really never 'spected you'ns to accept 'em."

"We will do what we can. Just understand that there may be a limit to what he can learn and how long he can stay in school." As Mr. Elder spoke, he stood up, grabbed the bell, then continued. "When that time comes, we'll let you know. It would be good if you would leave him with us today and let him get started."

Mama Wilson had earnestly prayed for Bud to be accepted. These teachers bent over backwards to help him. Bud could go to school! She believed an education would help him become independent, especially when she and Papa were gone.

Mrs. Elder lead her to the porch while Mr. Elder rang the class bell. Bud got in line to file in, as if he was already a class member. Mama Wilson watched. Her heart leapt as she watched her son walk to class.

***

For some reason, Mama Wilson felt down deep inside that Bud's being alone might come sooner than expected, since he had come along when she and Papa Wilson were much older.

As she headed home, she prayed, "Dear Lord, please allow Bud tuh learn readin'. You're his Father. He will grow in learnin' faith and love from the Shepherd, your Son, who leads him. In your Son's precious name, Amen."

CHAPTER FOUR

- HOME AT SCHOOL -
You shall be taught by the Lord.
~ Isaiah 54:13 (NKJV) ~

Bud, enjoyed school. He always took with him his ear-to-ear grin, and cheerful attitude. He began talking more, plus other ways of communicating.

On his first day of school, Mrs. Elder started teaching Bud the letters of the alphabet. "Ok Bud let's start with the letter 'A.' Can you say 'A.' Mrs. Elder opened her mouth wide dropping her jaw.

Bud repeated, "A---aa---den."

"Bud don't put "den" on the end of the letter. Ok?" Mrs. Elder instructed. She held up the letter B. "B, can you say B."

Bud repeated "B---ee---den."

Mrs. Elder smiled and exclaimed, "Good job Bud. 'B' is the letter your name starts with…B-U-D!"

Bud sounded it out, "Bbb---uuu---dd---den!" It made the other children happy to see him catch on.

Bud learned to recognize each letter of the alphabet, always saying "den" at the end. Mrs. Elder wasn't able to accomplish breaking Bud's habit.

Another problem Mrs. Elder had to address while teaching Bud was he never grasped how to leave a space between the letters or words when needed. For example, he would write "WARDWILSON," leaving out the needed spacing, plus always using capital letters.

"Students, today we will practice writing our first name on the board. When I call your name, go to the board, and write your name on the drawn lines: Issac, Jo Jo, Bud, and Daniel." Bud found his spot and slowly wrote "WARDWILSON."

"Bud, put a space between the D and W; like this---WARD WILSON." Mrs. Elder demonstrated the correct spacing.

"Wor---dah---We---ll---snn---den." He would pronounce, but write WARDWILSON. He couldn't grasp the concept.

When Bud wrote his name, the class would clap to encourage him. He just smiled his ear-to-ear grin.

Reading was another problem. Mrs. Elder tried everything she knew to do. Bud couldn't grasp how the sounds went together. She had the strong reading students read to Bud, hoping it would help. But still, all he would ever do was repeat what they read.

At reading time Bud could not understand letters making actual words. The only word he could read was his own name.

No matter what Mrs. Elder tried, He never grasped lower-case letters.

The entire year Mrs. Elder and the students worked hard to teach Bud to read and write more than just his name. At this time the process seemed to evade him. However, many years later, in a strange and miraculous way his year of schooling came to fruition. Another way in which God showed his sovereign plan for Bud.

***

Most classmates were kind to Bud. However, there were the usual school bullies who got their jollies from torturing someone different.

"Hey Bud---yous like Liz. Yous thinks she's purdy." Derk was the school bully, who shamed Bud with girlie remarks. "Kiss 'er Bud. Yous want to kiss 'er don't yah."

Liz, always Bud's protector, jumped in. "Stop it Derk! You shut up, or I'll tell the teacher." Bud just stood there. His grin, not so big.

"Go ahead, tell the teacher. I ain't scared." Derk spouted, laughing at Liz's defense of Bud. As Liz ran off to tell Mr. Elder, she grabbed Bud's hand pulling him with her. Knowing he was in trouble; Derk ran off to hide.

Mr. Elder came out on the porch calling, "Derk get up here, NOW! If you don't come now, I will pay a visit to your pa!" Derk came out from his hiding place behind the trees on the north side of the ball field. It was better to take licks from Mr. Elder then the thrashing his pa would give him if he found out about his meanness.

"Derk, what mean things did you say to Bud and Liz?" He took Derk by the arm, leading him to the Big Room.

"Not that bad. Liz is just a tattletale, Mr. Elder. I was just playin' with 'em." Derk lied.

"If you don't tell me the truth now, you will get paddled," exclaimed Mr. Elder.

Derk squirmed and became indignant, "Ahh, I's only teasin' 'em."

"That's it, Derk!" Mr. Elder shook his finger in Derk's face. "Now you will miss three recesses and write on the chalk board fifty times 'I will be kind to Bud.' If this ugly talk continues, you will force me to issue licks! Now get to it." He pushed him toward the board.

Mr. Elder didn't know Derk was bullying Bud after school as well. He chased Bud, throwing rocks at him. Bud couldn't run very fast, so Derk could catch him and shove him around till he cried.

"Ohh---sss---sto---pp---den, sss---sto---pp---den. Bud would cry. Derk stopped only when he wanted. Leaving Bud on the ground, he laughed hard as he left.

Two days later, Derk spouted off to his class mates as he pulled out a knife, "Today I'm gonna make Bud laugh like the clown he is!" Just then Mr. Elder rang the bell for class.

He took a step toward the kids squinting his eyes, "If any of you's get the notion to tell the teachers, I'll use this here sticker on yah!" As he spoke, he shoved the knife toward them.

After school, Derk ran Bud down. Pulling out his knife he started in, "How does you's like this Bud!" He held up the blade. Coming toward Bud he kept jabbing the knife. "Do you's see this 'ere blade? It's gonna' cut you's Bud."

"I'm gonna' make yous' laugh like the clown you is. With that big grin, you'd make a funny clown. So, let's hear you laugh, you clown, laugh."

***

God always had Bud's back.

***

Suddenly, rocks begin to whirl from every side, hitting Derk hard. From behind the trees came Liz, Kay, Arley, and Bill, Bud's friends from school, running and throwing large rocks hitting Derk hard.

"Ouch! Stop! It hurts!" Derk took off. While trying to block the rocks he dropped his knife.

Kay picked up the knife. "Tomorrow we'll show Mr. Elder this." She held up the knife. "It'll be the evidence we need to prove how Derk would have made Bud bleed."

Bud's friends gathered round him. Bill put his arm around Bud's shoulder. "Are you ok Bud? Come on Bud, we'll walk yah home."

"Waa---kkk---hoo---mm---den." Bud smiled his ear-to-ear grin with a thankful heart.

***

Mr. Wilson was surprised to see Bud's friends walking him home. They explained what had taken place. Showing him the knife, Bud's parents were horrified and concerned that Derk could be that mean. Bud's friends had saved him.

"Thank y'all fer helping Bud. He could have been badly hurt." Papa Wilson expressed his thanks. He took Bud's hand and turned him around to face him. "Bud, you must never again walk home alone."

"Mr. Wilson, every day we will take turns walkin' Bud home. He is our friend, and we want no harm tuh come tuh him." All of Bud's friends agreed with Bill.

Mama Wilson had to dry her eyes before she could speak. Pointing to the kitchen table she waved her hands, "Y'all have a seat. I jest made a batch of sugar cookies, and we have fresh goat's milk."

They all expressed their gratitude at the same time; "Thanks"; "Wow"; "Umm"; "These er good." But it was Mama Wilson who was grateful.

***

At school the next day, Bud's friends told Mr. Elder how Derk attacked Bud, Arley spoke first. "Mr. Elder, Derk's been bullyin' Bud. Not only at school, but on his walk home. Some of us seen this happenin', but was scaret to say anything 'cause Derk threatened us. He said if we told he would cut us."

Liz jumped in. "But yesterdee', he bragged to Bill that he was a-gonna use his 'sticker' to threaten Bud if'n he did'n bring him some tabackie from his Pa. We all decided to foller 'em, tuh see if he acted out his threat."

Bill finished the story, "We follered Derk in the woods alongside the road so's he couldn't see us. When he caught Bud, he pulled his knife on 'em. He was goin' to cut 'em! We came out fast throwin' rocks hittin' Derk so's he'd run!"

Mr. Elder was very quiet as his face grew red. Derk slid down in his seat. Steadily he walked over to Derk. Pulling him out of his desk by the knap of his neck he guided him to the front of the class. Pointing to the 'tardy' chair he exclaimed, "Derk sit down and don't move!"

"I'm very proud of you students for helping Bud. He could have been badly hurt. Because of your help you may have an extra recess. You are dismissed."

The students listened as Mr. Elder gave Derk swats. As the paddle landed hard, Derk yelped loudly, because at heart he was a wimp.

According to Derk's little brother, after Mr. Elder took Derk home and explained the situation to his pa, he received another thrashing. For a while it helped, but later he just started torturing Bud again.

Derk was suspended from school for the rest of the year.

***

It was as though Derk was put here on Earth to bully Bud. He never got away with his actions. He was always caught and punished. No one liked him. The more he hated Bud, the more he was hated, even by his own family.

It brings to mind the scripture ***Proverbs 11:21 (NIV): "The wicked will not go unpunished, but those who are righteous will go free."*** Exactly!

***

The last day of Bud's schooling, he was awarded a Certificate of Honor for his good character. Because of his ear-to ear-grin, the students voted him 'Zafra School's Happiest Student'.

Mrs. Elder tried teaching him the alphabet and how to write his name, but at this time he couldn't grasp the concept. Because there were no classes for students with disabilities, they had to let him go. The Elders did make it clear; Bud could visit any time.

***

It is ironic, Bud was not capable of learning much; but he taught everyone

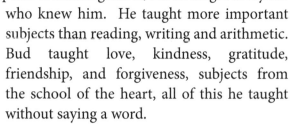

who knew him. He taught more important subjects than reading, writing and arithmetic. Bud taught love, kindness, gratitude, friendship, and forgiveness, subjects from the school of the heart, all of this he taught without saying a word.

God taught Bud; and to everyone he met, Bud taught God.

CHAPTER FIVE

- GROWIN' UP -

Grow in the grace and knowledge of our
Lord and Savior Jesus Christ.
~ II Peter 3:18 (ESV) ~

Mr. and Mrs. Elder sent a letter to the Wilsons:

Dear Mr. and Mrs. Wilson,

Thank you for the time we had with Bud as our student. He is kind and gentle, always smiling and eager to participate.

At this point in his education we believe he has learned all we have to offer. It is our opinion Bud should continue to practice writing his name, the alphabet and numbers. As he grows into an adult, he will possibly be able to read and write his name, as well as use numbers for simple addition and subtraction.

Each semester we will send educational materials to help him practice the alphabet, reading, and numbers.

He is always welcome at the school's events and functions.   He may visit anytime.

If you need our help, you only need to ask. Your family will always be in our prayers.

God's Blessings,
Mr. and Mrs. Elder
Zafra Public School

After Mama Wilson read the letter to Bud, she smiled, "You did well in school, but now I'll help you continue you's learnin."

"Ler---in---den," he copied.

"Every day we must work on you'rn writn' letters, readin' and numbers."

Bud's big grin expressed his excitement, "Wri---ten---den---ree---den---den."

A special place at the kitchen table was made for Bud to continue practicing his lessons. Every day after breakfast, Bud would try to make his letters and numbers, but he could not comprehend how to separate letters or words.

One day Mama Wilson thought of a new idea to help Bud learn.

"Bud let's play a game. Hows 'bout learnin' to write one of you'rn friend's name?"

Bud repeated, "Fri---en---duh---naa---mm---den."

"Let's start with your friend Bill. B-I-L-L." She slowly wrote out each letter. "Bill." She slid her finger across the bottom pronouncing the name.

Smiling, Bud pointed at the name and said "B-I-L-L---fri---en---duh---Bb---ii--lll---den." He got it! It was a break through!

"Bud, tomorrow we will practice writin' your friend June's name." Bud repeated, "Juu---nnn---den." If his grin would have gotten any bigger, it would have gone clear back into his ears.

***

Bud attended church, learning the stories of the Bible, playing with his friends, and helping his family with the farm. Sometimes they allowed him to visit school.

Every day Mama Wilson would practice the alphabet and numbers trying to teach him to write his name, and understand how to add and subtract.

In these early years, Bud took an interest in the Wilson's goat herd. He loved all the farm animals, but especially the goats. He named every goat in the herd. Till his dying day, he cared for and loved his goats.

Bud developed a relationship with his goats to the point it was as though they could talk to each other. Bud's goats never rejected, made fun of, or belittled him. Neither he nor his goats were judgmental toward each other. They developed a common bond. It was something special to behold.

***

About the time Bud turned nine, Mama Wilson became sick. She quickly grew weak becoming bedfast. Bud became her helper, waiting on her while Papa Wilson worked.

Every morning Bud asked, "Ma---ma—yho---oo---goo---da---den?"

"Doin' ok Bud. How er you this mornin'?" Mama Wilson never told Bud how sick she really felt. Bud gave his mama a sad look and touched her hand. "G---oo---da---den?"

"Fi---x---bre---kk---fst---den." He headed to the kitchen.

"Thank you's." She responded. "Just eggs Bud. Don't ferget tuh bring the medicine."

"Maa---deh---sss---en---den." Bud replied.

Bud finished preparing breakfast for Mama Wilson. He had become a pretty good cook. He propped her up, sat down beside her and fed her.

One day after she finished eating, she asked Bud to sit for a minute. "Bud---it's very important fer you's to understand I'll be leavin' here soon. Don't yah be scared now. I will go to be with the Lawd in heaven." Mama Wilson pointed up.

"When the time comes fer me tuh go, you're tuh help paw. Now that you'rn brother and sisters has left, you's the only one here tuh help 'em." She lay still shutting her eyes to gather her strength.

Taking a deep breath, she continued, "Bud, the most important thing yuh must remember is to love the Lord God, and Jesus, go to church and be a good boy." Tears started to slide down her cheek. "I love you Bud. You're smart. God has a purpose fer your life. Always remember He has a plan…," she stopped, out of breath.

Bud sat still holding on to Mama Wilson's hand until she went to sleep. Not quite sure what mama meant about her leaving. He gently took his hand away and quietly left the room. Tears replaced his ear-to-ear grin.

***

A few days later, very early in the morning, Bud woke to the sound of crying. Realizing it was papa, he ran to find him kneeling by mama's bed holding her hand.

"Bud, Mama Wilson's gone to be with the Lawd. I gotta go and get help. You's stay with her 'til I get back."

Bud ran to Mama Wilson's bedside. He screamed, "Mah---muh---mah---muh---den---dea---duh—den!" He rocked back and forth crying out her name.

Papa Wilson grabbed Bud's hands and held them. "Bud! Stop this here yellin' now! I must go fer help. Stop this yelling!' You's must take care of you'rn mama while I'm gone!"

Bud stopped. His moaning turned to prayer. Kneeling down, he took Mama Wilson's hand, gently stroking it he prayed; "O---Gah---duh---mah---muh---ha---van---den."

***

Bud had only seen one funeral. When he was younger, he went to a funeral where a small child by the name of Jimmy had died. He watched everyone cry as they filed by the casket.

Through the service, Bud thought he could help by smiling. As Bud followed his mama to view the body, he put his hand on the casket and said, "Hi---Jim---me---den." Bud didn't know not to talk to Jimmy. It made Mama Wilson and others cried harder.

That day Bud learned one thing; death is sad.

***

No grin was on Bud's face. Huge tears flowed down his cheeks. Bud knelt by Mama Wilson's bed 'til papa came with help.

Preston and Pastor Dalton consoled Papa Wilson and Bud saying, "You both know Mama Wilson loved the Lord and she was not afraid to leave you both in our hands. Now Ethel and Bertha will prepare her for the memorial service."

Ethel and Bertha washed Mama Wilson's body, dressed her in her Sunday best, which Papa picked out for her, and gently laid her on the bed.

The next day, Preston brought a large pine box he had carved for Mama Wilson's coffen. He and brother Dalton put her body inside.

The day of the service, several men from the congregation moved the pine box to the church house. The ladies from church brought huge bunches of flowers to sit around the pine box, and enough food for several days.

The sun was bright as though pronouncing: "Don't be sad, Mama Wilson is with the Lord, so smile!"

Pastor Dalton drove Bud and Papa Wilson to the church. All of Bud's sisters, brother and their families were there.

The church house was packed. Bud had never seen so many people in church before. He had a lot of hands to shake. As he shook each person's hand, he pronounced their names. "Ja---ree---den, Joh---on---den," etc.

The service began with Preston reading the obituary and a tribute to Mama Wilson.

"Today we are here to honor Mrs. Ura Johnson Wilson, better known to us as Mama Wilson. She is a most kind and gentle women. She and Papa Wilson have shown nothin' but love to their family, Ura B., Rosie, Nancy, Albert and Bud."

Preston's voice became shaky. "The Wilsons 'er good friends tuh us. Always helpful tuh anyone in need."

"Mama Wilson loves our Lord. She showed faith in the darkest time of her life, that bein' when Bud got lost. We had pert' near lost all hope, but not Mama Wilson."

"In those three long, scary days, we heard her pray, 'God, you know how it feels to have you'rn son gone tuh a strange place. A place of darkness like this 'ere old world. Now, my son is in a dark place. I knows you'll help us find 'em. Please bring 'em home.' And---He did!"

"Faith is what Mama Wilson lived by. A faith she always showed by her actions. A faith that is not an emotion; but a decision." Preston wiped his eyes and sat down.

Pastor Dalton moved to the podium. "Everyone stand and join in singin' Mama Wilson's favorite hymn, MY FAITH LOOKS UP TO THEE."

> *My Faith looks up to Thee,*
> *Thou Lamb of Calvary,*
> *Savior Divine.*
> *Now hear me while I pray.*
> *Take all my fears away.*
> *Oh, let me from this day,*
> *be holy Thine.*

(Lowell Mason – 1792-1872/Ray Palmer – 1808-1887)

Bud's singing was louder than usual. Everyone enthusiastically followed.

"Brother Lane, would you please pray?"

Brother Lane stood, cleared his throat, speaking softly, but with the power of the Spirit, prayed:

> *Oh God, our Father, we know this family is yours. You have protected their son Bud, and you have given them what they needed to sustain a prosperous life.*

He paused trying to control the tears:

> *You have Mama Wilson home with you. In her absence we employ your continued help for this family. May you protect and grant them much faith. May our community and church family support them, and comfort them with the comfort which only you provide. Help Papa Wilson, and his children to have faith in Thee, and may their sorrow turn to joy, and their joy be found in the fact she is now in your arms. In Jesus' Blessed and heavenly name, Amen."*

Pastor Dalton preached the sermon:

Today we celebrate the homecoming of our saint Mama Wilson. She was not a saint because she was perfect, but because she put her faith into action. She saw the Almighty's hand hold her son fer three days in these here mountain woods, lost in the dark, filled with the dangers of critters and beasts. A reminder of the three days God's Son was in the tomb. Due to her faith, and God's sovereignty, he was found!

He choked; pausing to gain control and continued:

After the victory of finding Bud, Mama Wilson never forgot what her Father had done for her. She believed! She stood on faith in God.

As John 14:1-3 (NIV) says:

Do not let your hearts be troubled.
You believe in God; believe also in me.
My Father's house has many rooms;
If that were not so, would I have told you
that I am going there to prepare a place for you?

And if I go and prepare a place for you,
I will come back and take you to be with me
that you also may be where I am.

Pastor Dalton took a deep breath pressing into the pulpit saying:

Already Mama Wilson is in her house the Father built for her and in the presence of Jesus, her best friend; her Savior.

If any of you have not given your heart to the Savior, who I just quoted--- 'Let not your heart be troubled,' meaning you can be free of heart trouble, fear and worry; don't wait. Come to Jesus today. This would be the best way to honor Mama Wilson. We can hear her say, 'They were lost, but now they're found!'

Pastor Dalton raised his arms and said, "Let's stand as we sing the song of God's Amazing Grace."

The congregation never sang better. As Bud sang, his ear-to-ear grin returned.

***

As they lowered Mama Wilson's body into the ground, Thelma Lou took a flower from the casket piece. Handing it to Bud, she said, "Bud when they lower the casket to the bottom of the grave, throw the flower on top. Then tell you'rn mama goodbye."

As the men begin to shovel dirt into the dark hole, Bud stood at the edge and loudly exclaimed, "Bbb---i---mah---muh---den." As he said bye, his face lit up with his smile.

The Father's sovereign peace prevailed.

CHAPTER SIX

- MEETING BUD -
As water reflects the face,
so one's life reflects the heart.
~ Proverbs 27:19 (NIV) ~

Six Years Later

Bud looked in the mirror. "You're all grown up Bud." Papa Wilson smiled nodding his head in approval.

"Gr--oh---nuh---puh---den." Bud echoed, pushing down his pants leg trying to make it longer.

Papa Wilson drew in a big breath. "Bud, it's time yuh learnt tuh shave." He pointed to his face. "Look," he rubbed Bud's hairy cheeks. "This here's whiskers. You seen me shave. Now, it's you'rn time." Bud's eyes got big.

"Sha---vuh---den," he stammered. Scared to try, papa lent Bud a hand and together, Bud got his first shave.

***

On Sunday, Ethel handed Bud a large box. "Bud, the church got yuh some new clothes. You're gettin' bigger and your body is a changin'. All your clothes 'er too small. These here shirts and paints will fit and be more comfortable."

Bud smiled his big grin. "Buh---da----clo---ss---den." He thankfully took the box.

"Bud, you go put them in Pastor's pickup right now, so's you don't ferget 'em." Thelma Lou wasn't asking, she was demanding.

As he rounded the corner at the back of the church house, he heard Derk's voice and callous laugh. Seeing the entire gang, Bud ducked behind pastor's pickup. They were smoking and coughing, hiding behind the cars.

In the fence row behind the parking area was a bee's nest. A bee started after Bud. Swatting at him, he dropped the box. The noise startled the entire gang and they jerked around seeing Bud.

Derk immediately started in on his prey. The gang, consisting of Marilyn, Ted, and Bubba, followed, surrounding Bud. "Bud's got a girlfriend." The others laughed. "Who do you like Bud? Liz? Kay?"

"It's Liz." Marilyn scoffed. Marilyn was the only girl gang member. Most of the time, she would get the boys going, then back out while they clobbered someone. "Look! Here she comes."

Seeing Bud in trouble, Liz went straight to Derk and pushed him as hard as she could. "Stop this teasin'!"

Caught off guard, Derk started to shove back, "I'll show you!"

To everyone's surprise, Bud stepped in front of Derk stopping him cold. Bud was much bigger, and looking at Bud and not a girl, made Derk pause. It was Just enough of a delay. As Derk raised his fist, Pastor Dalton yelled, "Stop!"

"What is this?" Pastor Dalton spit out loudly as he came around the corner. The gang quickly threw down their smokes, smashing them.

"De---rk---mee---nah----den," (Derk mean) Bud spoke on his own, not repeating someone else's words.

"Derk and his gang was trying to hurt Bud." Liz announced through her tears. "I was tryin' to keep him from gettin' hurt."

"It wasn't me." Marilyn lied, trying to look sad and hide the truth. "Derk started it!"

Ted joined in. "We was just talkin' about goin' to summer church camp. Bud came over and Derk lit into 'em."

Derk's hand made a fist. "Ted is lyin' and so is Marilyn, all of us were in on it!"

Pastor Dalton's face turned bright red and he insisted, "All of yuh come with me. Liz, are you ok?" Blowing her nose, she nodded her head yes.

Around the corner came Papa Wilson. "What's goin' on here?" He saw there was trouble.

"Mr. Wilson, I'll tell yah later. You and Bud get in the pickup. I'll be just a minute."

Pastor Dalton headed the gang back around the corner to the front porch. He called their parents over to him and explained the situation. The parents reacted with embarrassment and alarm.

"Our youth outing is this comin' Saturday. Because of their meanness, they won't be allowed to go." He was stern and made no bones about restricting them. He turned to look Derk and the other gang members in the face. "If I catch you doin' anything like this again, or even hear of it, you will not go with the church youth anywhere the rest of this year. And, if necessary, I'll get the law involved!" With that, he turned and marched to his pickup.

For a time, the gang laid low. For a time, there was not another incident of them torturing Bud. However, the persecution would raise its ugly head again.

***

Pastor Dalton received a call to pastor a church in Kansas closer to his and his wife's, Ethel's, families. They believed God's will was for them to go. With much prayer they shared the news with the congregation.

"Friends, God has called us home. I don't mean Heaven! Three weeks ago, we received a letter askin' us to take Prairie Land Christian Church in Kansas. The church is not far from both of our families."

He paused to steady his voice.

"Leavin' all of you and our home here, won't be easy. Our love fer you will never dwindle." His tears kept flowing. "We'll be leavin' the last Sunday of this month."

There was no sermon with words in the church service that day; it was tears, hugs, words of love and prayers.

Soon after church, everyone had gone except Pastor Dalton and Bud. Bud shook Pastor Daltons hand. "Baa---d---pas---trr---Dah---el---ten---fre---nd---den."

"Yes, you will always be our friend Bud." Bud's ear-to-ear smile stretched so hard, it looked like it hurt. He knew Bud would never forget his family's names---and they would definitely not forget him.

The last Sunday of the month, every church member was there to hear Pastor Dalton's last sermon and to tell his church family goodbye, saying, "Today is not a sad day, but a happy day for my family and I. All of you know how much we've grown to love ya'll. Especially goin' through the time of startin' the church and buildin' this beautiful rock church house. We feel the love. But now, it's time to move on. A new pastor and his family are on their way."

God said:

To everything there is a season,
and a time for every purpose under heaven..."
~ Ecclesiastes 3:1 (NKJV) ~

You could hear the sniffles, as emotion brought tears.

"Know you will be in our constant prayer. Please, keep us in your prayers. Remember, we are all kinfolk through the blood of our Lord Jesus Christ."

Looking at Bud, he motioned for him to come and stand by him. Bud jumped up and walked forward, his usual, fast pace---stopping close to Pastor Dalton.

"Our family has one final request, a top priority for all of ya'll. That's why I have asked Bud to stand beside me. We ask you all to take care of our Bud. Papa Wilson is gettin' older, the church family must help meet their needs. Please honor our final request!"

The congregation begin to clap. They all stood in commitment. Ethel and the children joined him on stage. The clapping continued for several minutes.

Pastor Dalton waved his hands to silence the congregation. "Love your neighbor as yourself. Not my command; the Lord's command." With that the service ended.

After the fellowship dinner, everyone said their farewells, waving as the family left headed to their new home.

***

One week later the new pastor's family arrived. His name was Abraham, but everyone called him Abe. His wife's name was Kerri, a beautiful lady who sang and played the piano. They had two girls; Ann, four, and Marie, two.

Pastor Abraham and his family came from Dallas, Texas. Were they ever in for a surprise! The rugged mountain area of Zafra would take some getting used to. Rough, pothole dirt roads made travel difficult. Some of the neighbors had no electricity; living in a house with dirt floors and no windows or doors. Most homes were two- or three-room dwellings. Their floors had large cracks between each board. Heat came from a big iron wood stove; cool came from having no windows or doors. Besides the dogs and cats, sometimes even the chickens lived in the house.

The country store stocked basic staples, plus candy, ice cream and pop. Gas wasn't available. Gas was a good ten miles away.

The church still used outdoor toilets. Using an outdoor toilet was an adventure. In the winter, you froze. In the summer, you fought off the snakes and bugs. Toilet paper was the *Sears, Roebuck & Co.* catalog.

Though rugged it was beautiful. Trees of hard wood, cedar, and pine rose stately covering the region. Cliffs, rocky hills, winding rivers, crystal clear creeks and streams wound their way through the valley. Every kind of wild flower, fruit and berry covered the woods and the hills.

Moonshine was a problem; indulgence of both men and women caused drunkenness, ignited abuse, and sometimes death. Moonshine kept some in trouble with the law and others clothed and fed. But mostly it was a medicine for healing snakebites, wounds, stomach trouble and influenza.

Tobacco use started with young children around the age of five or six. It was not thought of as harmful, but a deterrent for bad teeth and worms.

Hunting and fishing fed a family. Youngest to oldest shared the skill of bringing in wild game. Every part of the animal was used to feed and clothe their families. Killing an animal was not sport, but survival.

Everyone grew a garden. If anyone lost their crop, all the neighbors would share what they grew. Canning and smoking meat was done in the summer to provide for winter food.

The culture of these mountain people ran deep. Independent, hard workers, lovers of family and country, and most adults had little or no education, perseverance is the description of their strong character and heart.

Soon after arriving Pastor Abe and his family began to understand these mountaineers. It was in this place Pastor Abe and his family met Bud.

***

The first Sunday for the new pastor and his family, the church had a 'Meet & Greet' welcome breakfast. The family was in a receiving line for everyone to meet and shake hands, then continue through the food line. Bud was first in line.

Bud could appear a bit "scary," especially to a child. As a four-year-old, Ann saw a very tall, black-haired, misshaped face, bug-eyed, large protruding mole, an ear-to-ear grin, showing dirty yellow teeth and red raw gums man! On top of that, his smell was atrocious, clothes dirty. His breath would cause a person to hold theirs.

When meeting Bud for the first time Ann hid behind her dad's leg hanging on for dear life. Kerri grabbed Marie up into her arms. Bud walked up too close and, as usual, stuck out his hand.

34

Grabbing Pastor Abe's hand, shaking it hard, he began to speak, "Uh—uh—uh—Buh---da---den." Before he would release Pastor Abe's hand, he had to hear his name. "Hi. I'm Pastor Abe. Did you say your name is Bud?"

"Buh---da---Will---sss---n---paa---sss---ter---Aa---buh----den."

"Bud, this is my wife Kerri, and my daughters Ann and Marie." Bud tried to shake everyone's hand, but Ann wouldn't let go of her papa's leg, and Kerri held on tightly to Marie.

"KK---ree---Aa---nuh---Mah---ree---den. Their names would never be forgotten. As Bud spoke, all the "scary" waned. As he repeated each name, his eyes lit up. Kindness beamed through. All of his ugly physical characteristics disappeared behind his humility. Everyone who shook his hand felt important; to Bud they were. It was known as the "Bud Miracle!"

***

The first day was the last day the pastor's family was scared of Bud. It never again mattered how he looked, what he wore or how he smelled. Because, to Bud, no one mattered more than everyone.

Both the Father and His child Bud knows our names.

CHAPTER SEVEN

- BUD'S FAMILY: CHURCH -
God chose the lowly things of this world
and the despised things...
~ I Corinthians 1:28 (NIV) ~

Even in bad weather, Bud was a faithful church attendee. He lived back in the woods, about six miles from the church. Pastor Abe and his pickup truck with sideboards made the church bus run. The run was about a twenty-mile, round trip through the communities of Beachton and Zafra.

The kids rode in the back; the mothers in front. Going over those rough dirt roads, bouncing around, dust blowing in from every direction, so, by the time they reached the church house, everyone had to clean up.

Bud would head to shake hands with Pastor Abe, his wife and the girls. "Paa---sss---ter--- Aa---buh---den." He always said their name.

Pastor Abe was extra kind and gentle with Bud, giving him a Bible, although he knew he couldn't read, picking him up for church and taking Bud and Papa Wilson to town for doctor's appointments and groceries.

Bud always carried his Bible to church. He had help finding the chapters and verses that were being studied, carefully following along, mimicking how others were looking in the Bible. When they turned a page, Bud turned a page.

Missing a church trip, was not an option for Bud. If the bus was late, he would start walking, because he knew someone from church would be on their way to the event and he could catch a ride.

Friday night was church "Skate Night." Even though He couldn't skate, he never missed. Mostly, he shook hands, ate popcorn and drank soda pop.

Youth Rally's took place once a month. Each church was invited to bring special music. When the minister announced for Zafra Church to come up, Bud headed to the platform. One of his favorite gospel hymns to perform was *When I See the Blood*.

He lifted his head, rocked back and forth, and sang loudly:

> *Ben—n—ah---sse---deh---bud---da*
> *(When I see the Blood.)*
>
> *Ben—n—ah---sse—deh---bud---da*
> *(When I see the Blood.)*
>
> *Ben---n—ah---sse—deh---bud---da*
> *(When I see the Blood.)*
>
> *Ah---un---pa—sss---o—per---hoo—da*
> *(I will pass, I will pass over you.)*

A loud round of applause always followed his performance. It was as if those listening heard his singing miraculously changed from off-key to inspirational.

***

Every Sunday Ann and Bud joined together in singing. She was five and, in his mind, so was Bud. Ann and Bud became partners when it came to bellowin' out the hymns.

One Sunday morning when their duet was going strong, Grace, the nosy lady of the church, scolded Bud and Ann. "You two are just a little loud. Could you please turn it down a notch? Singing should be pleasant."

Smiling his special grin, Bud repeated her name. "Gah---rasss---den," sticking out his hand for her to shake as he stuttered out her name. Ann started to cry.

Ignoring Bud's hand, she turned and walked off in a huff, heading to her seat. Grace was a constant unhappy complainer. Especially about others singing. She considered herself a refined and studied vocalist, making her a self-proclaimed vocal judge.

Grace's talking-to didn't affect Bud. In fact, his singing got louder. For a time, Ann toned it down. But eventually, she got over being scolded and joined Bud. She told her papa, "The Bible says 'Make a joyful noise'" and Bud and her did exactly that!

***

Bud began to believe he had the responsibility to help serve in the church. For years he had watched the other adults and he wanted to be involved like they were.

The church was overflowing with young children, many whose parents didn't attend. Plus, some parents who were there ignored their children's disruption of the worship service. Somehow, Bud decided he needed to help in that area as church disciplinarian.

When the disruption started, he would get up and walk over to the child, put his hands on their shoulders, march them to their seat, sit them down, and hold them there until they became still.

"Sh---sh---shhhhh." Bud was serious. There was no ear-to-ear grin on his face.

If they got out of their seat again, Bud would get them by the arm, take them back and set them down hard. If that didn't work, he would sit down by them.

For a while, it worked. Until one Sunday, Bud happened to scare a child he tried to correct. The child started to cry.

After services, Mrs. Sharp, the child's mother, headed for Pastor Abe. "If Bud keeps botherin' my kids, we won't be attendin' church here no more," she yelled. "Bud's got no right to get on tuh my kids. He scares 'em. I want him tuh stop!"

"Yes, I understand Mrs. Sharp. Bud's just trying to help. I'll have a talk with him. You and your children need to be a part of our church family. Soon, they'll be teenagers. Here is where they learn God's Word. I will explain to Bud how you and I will take care of the children."

Mrs. Sharp teared up. "I know my kids ain't perfect. They's uh little fearful of Bud. I know he don't mean them no harm. But it's better if you or I get on to 'em."

Pastor Abe talked to Bud. "Bud, we have a problem and I need your help."

Bud's eyes got big, as he smiled his ear-to-ear grin. "Ha---ll---pa---den." Bud was always ready to serve.

"Yes. Instead of helping with the children during the service, I need you to help sit up the classrooms and hand out the weekly announcements."

"Claa---ss---roo---mm---ann—now---sss—mun---sss---den." His ear-to-ear grin grew. The new assignment satisfied him.

Pastor Abe had a life-time helper and Mrs. Sharp and her brood stayed in church.

***

Bud never missed a "Pot-luck" fellowship dinner. Could he ever eat! Bud was always first in line. He was a master at filling his plate to the nth degree. He would return for a fill up two, three, or sometimes four times.

At every dinner, Bud would tell the cooks, "Umm---goo---uh---dah---den."

The women of the Church loved seeing Bud eat their cooking. New recipes were tried out on Bud. All the women appreciated Bud eating anything and everything. He never threw away the food.

Mrs. Shepherd, a kind, chunky, church lady, always encouraged Bud, "Eat up Bud; reckon we've got plenty." "Pl---an---nee---den," Bud replied with his mouth full.

The Zafra Church fellowship dinners were famous throughout the area, because the women cooked their best homemade dishes just to watch Bud eat.

***

Ever since she was born, Ann had been hearing her father's sermons. Her love for Jesus grew and grew. She always knew Him.

As her father preached about His love, grace, and the message of salvation, she felt it was time for her to follow what the Bible said.

Pastor Abe preached, "Jesus said, 'Let the little children come to me, for such is the kingdom of heaven.' To be His, all we must do is humble ourselves, believe, repent, confess our sins and be baptized." Every sermon Pastor Abe included the plan of salvation.

"Baptism represents the death, burial and resurrection of our Lord, Jesus Christ. At baptism the gift of the Holy Spirit is received. After baptism, we are to walk in the Spirit's Light of Truth and Love."

He pleaded, "If you've never accepted Him, don't wait. Come today."

At five years of age, Ann knew Jesus wanted her to come. If Jesus wanted her to come, it was time. To herself she thought, "Jesus is my best friend. I'm ready. I'm giving my life to Jesus."

The very next Sunday at invitation time, Ann stepped out in the isle and walked toward her father. With tears in his eyes he stepped down from the pulpit and took her hand.

A sudden movement from the back of the church caused Pastor Abe to look up. Coming down the aisle were the Smith twins, Helen and Ellen. These girls had been attending the church since they were born. Now, they were 12 and accepting Jesus as their Lord and Savior.

As Pastor Abe took their hands, there was another commotion. Mrs. Daisey, came out of her pew and walked over to Bud, leaned down and started talking to him.

Now, Daisey could not whisper. When she tried to whisper, it came out louder than just her normal speaking voice. Everyone could hear what she said. "Bud, if you want tuh accept Jesus, go ahead." Bud ran down the aisle. If Jesus was calling him, he wasn't waiting!

Touched by all these children coming to the Lord, sounds of crying began to fill the room.

"As I said before, Jesus said, 'Let the little children come to me. Here they are: Ann, Helen, Ellen, and Bud. Age is not an issue when it comes to being a child of God; obedience is."

He took all their hands in his, and had them face him. "I have only two questions to ask you. Do you believe Jesus is the Christ the Son of the living God?"

In unison, the girls answered, "Yes."

Bud echoed, "Yea---sss---den."

Pastor Abe continued, "Do you want to accept Him as your personal Lord and Savior?"

Again, in unison the three answered, "Yes."

Bud echoed, "Yea---sss---den."

Pastor Abe, "Please repeat after me. I Believe..."

"I believe..."

Bud, "I---be---lee---va---den..."

Pastor Abe, "...that Jesus is the Christ..."

"...that Jesus is the Christ..."

Bud, "...th---tuh---Jee---uss---iss---tuh---ah---Ca---ri---sss---tuh---den..."

Pastor Abe, "...the Son..."

"...the Son..."

Bud, "...th---eh---Sss---on---den..."

Pastor Abe… "…of the living God."

"…of the living God."

Bud, "…off---th---uh---li---ven---Gah---duh---den."

Ann, Helen, Ellen and Bud…all God's children: one, age five; two, age twelve; and one, age twenty-six.

***

Everyone gathered at the Cow Creek baptistry. As the congregation stood on the bridge singing "Shall We Gather at The River"; Pastor Abe had them all take hands, then he took Ann's hand and they walked into the water.

Pastor Abe raised his right hand to heaven, "I now baptize you for the remission of your sins, in the name of the Father, Son and the Holy Spirit."

As each child came up out of the water, from the bridge the congregation sang *Now I Belong to Jesus*:

> *Now I belong to Jesus,*
> *Jesus belongs to me.*
> *Not for the years of time alone,*
> *But for eternity.*

(Norman J. Clayton 1903-1992)

***

From above Jesus and the angels watched. They all rejoiced. Jesus told them, **"Let the little children come to Me, and do not forbid them; for of such is the kingdom of heaven."** *(Matthew 19:14 – NKJV)*

43

CHAPTER EIGHT

- FINDING HOME -
...and a little child shall lead them.
~ Isaiah 11:6 (NKJV) ~

Papa Wilson's health begin to decline. He was starting to experience trouble eating and sleeping. Food didn't taste well; he began to lose weight and energy. He became tired and had no desire to be active.

"I miss mama," Papa Wilson told Bud. "It will soon be time fer me to go to mama." "Mah---muh---den." Bud repeated without his usual grin.

After Papa Wilson had stayed in bed two days, Bud decided he should get Pastor Abe. "Pah---puh---Buh---du---go—get---Pass---ter---Aa---buh---den." No response came from Papa Wilson.

Bud walked the six miles to Pastor Abe's house. Knocking hard on the door, Pastor Abe opened it, surprised to see Bud. "Well hello Bud; come on in. How are you? What's going on?" It was obvious something was terribly wrong.

Scared, Bud's voice went high and loud, "Co---mm---Pah---pah---sss---kkk---den." He grabbed Abe's shirt and pulled him toward the door.

"Ok Bud. I'll go with you. Kerri!" He yelled. She came running around the corner surprised to see Bud. "Kerri, Bud says Papa Wilson's sick."

Following them to the car she tried to reassure Bud. "We'll pray Bud. Don't worry. Abe is going with you."

***

The instant Abe saw Papa Wilson he knew it was critical. He sat beside him, leaning down to his ear. "Papa Wilson, Bud says you're not feeling well."

44

In a weak voice grasping for air, Papa Wilson replied, "I'm sick. Need to fetch me to Doc Redman."

"I'll go get help. Bud take care of Papa. When we get back, we'll be going to the hospital."

Bud sat by Papa's bedside. "Pah---pah---den---nah---ttt---fee---ll---goo---da---den."

Papa looked at Bud. "I'm tired son, and I miss mama."

Bud closed his eyes and prayed, "Gah---dh---Pah---puh---sic---kuh---hel---puh---Pah---pah---den."

Pastor Abe got back quickly bringing Preston with him. Bud kept holding Papa Wilson's hand while the men put him in the car.

Suddenly, Papa Wilson lifted his head speaking softly, "Bud---Bud can you hear me."

Bud cried, "Pa—Pa---den."

"Yah know I love yah Bud. Yuh must move out from these woods----so yuh won't---be alone." Grasping for air, his head went down.

Putting Papa Wilson's head in his lap, Bud leaned down with his ear close to Papa's mouth as he was trying to speak, "Bud---stay in church---they will---take care---of yah---love yah---son."

Slowly, and with all the strength he could muster, he lifted his hand patting Bud on his head. His hand dropped.

Leaning over the front seat, Preston took Papa Wilson's hand and felt for a pulse. No results. Preston touched Abe's arm getting his attention. "He's dead," he mouthed to Abe. Not realizing he was gone, Bud kept holding Papa's head.

***

As the paramedics came to take Papa Wilson out of the car into the emergency room, Bud begin to cry rocking hard back and forth. "Pah-

45

---puh---Pah---puh---den." Pastor Abe took Bud's hand from Papa Wilson's pulling him out of the car, so Papa's body could be moved.

"Bud, Papa Wilson has gone to heaven to be with Mama Wilson. We know he is so excited to see her again. He knows you will be ok, because we will take good care of you."

Continuing to hold Bud's hand, he sat him down. Over and over Bud rocked back and forth crying, "Pah---puh---Pah---puh---den!

Preston knelt beside him. "Bud, let's ask God fer help. Dear Lord, we are here with Bud your child. We ask you to please calm him. Allow him to feel your loving arms around him. In Your precious name, Amen." As Preston prayed, Bud settled down.

Pastor Abe waved his hand toward the sky. "Bud, listen! Now your Papa is there with God, Jesus, and Mama Wilson. They're showing him where he will live, and introducing him to the heavenly family."

Bud repeated the words, "Pah---puh---hea---van---lee---hoh---ma---den." Slowly a smile crept across his face. Their prayer was answered as the Father brought understanding to quiet Bud's heart.

***

The day of Papa's memorial service was bright and sunny. Bud had on his ear-to-ear grin. He smiled as though he knew something no one else knew. Bud's peace was not of this world, it was the peace that only Jesus brings.

The congregation sang Papa Wilson's favorite hymns; *I'll Fly Away* and *How Beautiful Heaven Must Be*. Bud and Ann sang at the top of their lungs. Whether the miracle was in Bud's voice or the listener's ear, no one knew, but Bud's loud singing sounded heavenly.

Pastor Abe shared how Papa Wilson loved his family. "Bud and his papa lived together, working hard to make ends meet. Papa Wilson saw to it that Bud attended every church event, never missing a service."

"Papa knows we'll take care of our Bud." He looked straight at Bud and stepped down from the pulpit.

"Bud, please stand." He took Bud's hand. "Today I want you to turn around and look at your new family." Bud turned and grinned. "All of you who'll be Bud's family and help him in all the ways a family helps its members, please stand."

As one big gust of wind, sounding like a roar, the entire congregation stood. If it was possible, Bud's ear-to-ear grin got bigger. Then, one clap, another, then more, until the entire congregation was clapping and shouting, "Praise God! Hallelujah! Yes Lord!"

***

The church is the heart and hands of God. God never does what His church should do. The church is all about family. The family of God is a place where the least person you want to live with always lives. That's because the church is the body of Christ with many parts. His love is shown through Her.

For the rest of Bud's earthly life, he lived with the church family.

***

While the church family took care of Bud's physical needs, he, by his actions, would nurture in them spiritual needs. Through Bud, God's sovereign love and compassion found its way into the fellowship of believers. As a whole, the Zafra Church never grasped this truth.

God's sovereignty was displayed through a nobody man of limited mind, in a place of no importance.

CHAPTER NINE

- A PLACE FOR BUD -
Jesus said, "...do not worry about your life, what
you will eat or drink; or...what you will wear..."
~ Matthew 6:25 (NIV) ~

Even though Bud was now 40 years old, he could not live alone. His nearest neighbors were six miles away. It was not safe. Now that all of his siblings had moved away and had families of their own, it wasn't possible for Bud to live with them.

A safe place for Bud needed to be found. Pastor Abe and Kerri took it upon themselves to find that place.

On Sunday, Abe explained the situation, "Kerri and I realize Bud needs a home in this community near the church. Living' alone in the woods is not an option. We need everyone's help to find a place for Bud."

Kerri spoke up, "We not only need to find him a place, but arrange his house so he can take better care of himself. Plus, find a place to move his goat herd. Please pray for this effort. Asking God for help is the way to get Bud a home and meet his needs."

Taking her hand, Pastor Abe prayed, "Oh Lord, bless this effort. Put it on our hearts to help settle Bud in this community. Open the flood gates of heaven in this search. You Lord hold all of this in your nail-scared hands. We pray for your guidance and direction. In your precious Son's name, amen.

With enthusiasm the Spirit of God filled the room. Immediately, everyone began discussing how they could help.

***

An older lady in Zafra who took in foster children, Mrs. Reddie Hodge, heard about Bud's situation. She was somewhat considered affluent in the community, because she and her husband owned the grocery store and, for the area, lived in a nice home.

Even though she was not a Christian, nor ever attended the church's social functions, she had a big heart for those in need. Sovereignty is visible even in unbelievers.

Mrs. Hodge's had a strong personality. She made no bones about what she wanted and how she thought things should be. Her language was sometimes offensive. However, if she wanted to talk to a person she liked, who didn't appreciate her adjectives, her language instantly cleaned up.

As the news of Bud's dilemma got around to Mrs. Hodge, she took immediate action. Pastor Abe got a call.

"Hello, Pastor Abe speaking."

"Hello Abe, this is Reddie Hodge."

"How are yo…" She interrupted. "Could you come over? What I have to say needs to be face-to-face." Mrs. Hodge never wanted to talk much over the phone due to the "party lines" always having nosey listeners, who, when they heard the ring, would pick up and listen in.

"Yes, I could come later this afternoon around four. Would that work for you?"

"Fine. Now, don't you forget. This is important. Be here on time. I can't tolerate tardiness." She commanded.

"Of course, I will be there. If I'm going to be detained, I'll call. Goodbye." As he hung up, he smiled knowing she would be a great help in finding a house for Bud. "Thank you, Lord," he prayed.

∗∗∗

As Pastor Abe drove over to Bud's to explain how his being alone made him extremely vulnerable to human predators and he couldn't live in his house anymore, he prayed Bud would understand. Bud also needed to know his animals would move with him. How this would work out was the question. The unknown could be scary. He would explain to Bud how faith is the answer.

"Pas---sss---ter---Aaa---bb---den." Bud stuck out his hand before Abe was even out of the pickup. He was always happy to see Pastor Abe.

"Bud, I need to talk with you. Could we sit on the porch?"

Pastor Abe prayed as he started to explain.

"Since Papa went to heaven, and you don't have any family members close by, we want to move you closer to the Church, into the community and by our family." He hoped Bud understood his words.

Bud looked around, then back to Pastor Abe. He said, questionably, "Moo---vh---den?"

"I promise all your animals will move with you. You'll be able to see them and feed them every day." As he spoke, he looked Bud straight in the eye.

Looking around for a moment, as if taking it all in, Bud responded. "Pas---ss---ter---Aa---bb---Bah---da---fr---ee---nd---den," and smiled his huge, ear-to-ear grin, meaning he agreed.

"Bud, Kerri's helping you move. She will pack up the house, while the church men gather your animals." He took hold of Bud's shoulders. "You and your animals will have a new home."

"Ba---duh---frr---en---Ker---ree---go—oo---wi—th---he—rr---den" He's eyes showed he understood exactly what Pastor Abe was saying.

"When Kerri gets your home items packed and the men move some of your furniture, we plan to move your house to a new location close to us and the church house."

Pastor Abe didn't tell Bud there wasn't a house place yet, because he had faith God would provide.

"Ok Bud! I'll go get things rollin' and be back later. Get your chores done, because Kerri will be here shortly to help you start packing." Bud's ear-to-ear grin stayed on his face as Pastor Abe drove off.

Bud's smile was the smile of a little child; his faith, like a grain of mustard seed. He never doubted that Pastor Abe, Kerri, nor the church family would take care of him.

***

Pastor Abe knocked on Mrs. Hodge's door. She yelled, her voice crusty with age, "Come on in!"

As he stepped inside, she immediately began her instructions. "Have a seat young man." She pointed to the big easy chair. "Would yuh like some ice tea or water?"

"No, thank you."

Mrs. Hodge leaned back in her chair. "I heard through our community 'grape vine,' Bud needs a house place. A place where no harm can come to him. You understand this?" She wasn't asking for an answer; she commanded one.

"Yes ma'am." Pastor Abe responded. This woman was no nonsense!

"I just left Bud's home where I spoke with him about the situation. To the best of his ability, he said we were his friends and he would move. The toughest part is finding a place for both his animals and his house."

Mrs. Hodge relaxed, "Well, good. You've done the right thing. You and Kerri work out the animal issue. I have land for Bud's house. Once we have him in his house, it will be my responsibility to be his caregiver."

"On Sunday, he will be with his church family. Throughout the week my granddaughter and I will help him with his house work, food and keeping clean." Again, she wasn't asking; she was telling.

Abe couldn't believe his ears. With Bud's house moved to this spot of land, all that was left to be done was find a home for his goats.

Mrs. Hodge gave a winsome grin, then continued. "I have an acre of land sittin' by Cow Creek Bridge across from the main road, close to where you do you'rn baptizin'. Bud can have it to sit his house on." She crinkled her brow as she seemed to be studying the situation.

"The men from the Brushy Ridge Community Church are willing to move the house. They own the equipment and will move it for free." Abe said with a smile.

God's mighty hand was putting things together. A place to live, completely free, given by someone nobody would expect. God is good all the time; all the time God is good!

Mrs. Hodge looked away, so he couldn't see the emotion in her face. She knew God was directing all of this, but she wouldn't admit it.

Pastor Abe stood up, sticking out his hand. "Mrs. Hodge thank you so much for your kindness. I'll head out to explain to the men we are ready to move Bud's house." They shook hands; her grip hard, her hands rough.

Still holding her hand, Abe paused. "May I pray with you."

When he said this, her eyes opened wide with surprise, "Why sure." She smiled. "Thank yah."

Still holding her hand and bowing his head, he prayed. "Dear Lord, may all our plans be your will. Thank you for Mrs. Hodge, her kindness and her desire to help those in need. May our plans work out to honor and glorify you. In Your Son's precious name, Amen."

When pastor Abe opened his eyes, Mrs. Hodge had tears flowing down her stern face. Quickly turning her head, she wiped them away. "You better get gone, we both got things to do."

"Good day Mrs. Hodge. Again, thank you." He headed out the door.

***

Kerri was also on task. Abe had shared with her the good news. Now it was her turn. She knew just the person who could and would help; Ada Chatham. The most kind and generous woman you ever met.

Ada was a true pioneer woman and a fine Christian. She was a widow lady, and owned over three-hundred acres of rich bottom land surrounded by the Mountain Fork River. Mrs. Ada's husband had died many years ago and she lived with her son Bobby.

Ada had every kind of farm animal available: pigs, chickens, cattle, cats and dogs, but no goats. Bud's goats would be a perfect addition to her farm. Goats kept pastures fertilized and replaced the hard work of brush hogging the land.

When Kerri honked her horn, Ada quickly came out the front door. "Come on in," she motioned. As she smiled, snuff rolled down both sides of her mouth. She always had a little hanky in her hand to quickly wipe it away, thinking no one would notice she dipped snuff.

"Hi Ada. Came to talk to you for a minute. You got time?" Kerri stepped on the porch and started through the door.

"Shor do. Sit here. Hows 'bout a glass of sweet ice tea. Made fresh this mornin'." Not listening for an answer, she headed off to get the tea.

"Sounds great! It's been a hot morning." Kerri raised her voice to answer while looking around the small house. Every window was open letting in the flies, floors were dirty, and ragged furniture gave it a comfortable flare. Hospitality oozed out all around.

From the kitchen, Ada hollered. "What's goin' on that's so important you'd come over?" She hurried in, handing Kerri the tea and sat down. Praying for exactly the right words, Kerri explained.

"I'll get straight to the point. We have decided to bring Bud out of the woods to live in the community. He must have a safe place where we can look after him. Mrs. Hodge donated land by Cow Creek to put Bud's house. Some of the loggers from the Brushy Ridge Community Church have offered to move his house over to the acreage." Kerri took a deep breath. "Now all that's needed is a place for his goats." Kerri paused, praying.

Ada smiled. Again, snuff oozed out from both sides of her mouth. She spit before she spoke, which was a good sign. "Bud don't need tuh be alone in them woods. He needs to be where no harm can come to 'em. Fer heaven's sake, of course he can, I got lots of room fer them goats."

Before Mrs. Ada could take a breath, Kerri jumped up and gave her a big hug. "Thank you, Mrs. Ada. Now I'm sure Bud will be glad to move, because his animals can come with him."

"How many of them their goats does Bud have?" Mrs. Ada asked.

"He's got twenty goats and two pigs. From here to where his house will sit is approximately three miles. Bud can walk here every day to feed and take care of them. Thank you, Ada. Your help is an answer to our prayer." Kerri hugged her again. "You're such a blessing and I dearly love you. I can't wait to tell Abe."

She quickly headed out the door.

"Yuh don't need to be in such a hurry; stay and talk fer awhile?"

"Next time I promise to stay longer. Best be gettin' back to share the good news. Abe's waiting. As soon as he hears, he will notify the men who will be moving the house. Bye, bye. God's blessings to you Mrs. Ada."

As she drove off, Kerri waved out the window, then began singing at the top of her lungs; "God is so good; God is so good. God is so good. He's so good to everyone."

***

A place for Bud was found. He had a new home, close to adopted family, friends and community. The house was moved by Cow Creek (the Zafra Church's baptistry); his animals were at their new home (Ada's three-hundred-acre farm), plus Mrs. Reddie Hodge would care for him. His mighty right hand fitting all the pieces together.

***

The righteous will never be uprooted… (Proverbs 10:30 - NIV)

CHAPTER TEN

- BUD'S GOATS -

...give careful attention to your herds.
~ Proverbs 27:23 (NIV) ~

Living on Mrs. Ada's 300-acre farm, Bud's goat herd was never so healthy. In the goat world, these goats were not anything special. They were a mixture of breeds and colors called *Brush Goats*. None of this mattered to Bud. He loved his goats.

When nannies died after having their kids, Pastor Abe was there to help Bud. He would bring them home to his daughters and their job was to bottle feed them until they were old enough to survive on their own.

Twice a day, morning and evening, the girls fed the babies. In late morning, Bud would stop by on his way back from feeding his goats on Ada's farm.

If the goats were in the middle of their bottle feeding and suddenly stopped and started bawling, Ann and Marie knew Bud was coming up the hill to their home. The minute he got to the barn, they would run and jump all over him. They thought Bud was their mama come back to life.

Bud hardly ever had anything to say to the girls, but the kids he would talk to in their own language. The kids would carry on with sounds of "baa," loud then soft, or high then low, or short then long. Ann and Marie would just stand in awe of the conversation.

***

One morning Ann and Marie were going horseback riding. They were just about to leave when Abe called out to them. "While you girls are out riding, I need for y'all to check on Bud's goats. I've got a men's meeting at the church and can't get over there today."

"Ok Papa," Ann said as she mounted her horse.

Walking over to the girls he warned them. "Be very careful. I was told there are wild dogs in this area. They're killers and have been spotted by several neighbors. They got into Floyd's chickens. He tried shooting them, but they got away. Apparently, it's a pack of three, and they are vicious."

"If you come across these dogs, don't get off your horses. One of you stay, scare them off and protect the goats. They will probably run off 'cause they're scared of humans. The other should go get help. Ada or I can help."

"We will Papa," they assured him.

He turned and headed to his car, stopped and called back, "Girls, the goats are in the north pasture."

The girls headed Jinx and Red down the hill toward Cannie Creek Road, which lead to the north pasture. Their horses were slow and laid back. "I hope we don't run into those dogs," Marie admitted. "Sounds scary."

"Me too," Ann agreed. "If they attack the goats, it'll be hard to fight them off. If they get a taste of blood it will be impossible. Once they taste blood there's no stopping them. We must be ready. Marie, let's ask God to help us."

They both looked up; Ann prayed, "God please protect the goats and us from the dogs. In Jesus' name, amen."

It was a beautiful day. The north pasture was about a 15-minute ride from home. The girls enjoyed the ride. Jinx and Red were always slow walking away from the barn, but fast on the way back, because back at the barn they knew they would get fed.

The girls kept their eyes and ears open looking out for the dogs.

About half a mile from the north pasture Marie exclaimed, "Look, there's Bud." Bud was coming down the road to check on his goats. Bud gave them his ear-to-ear grin.

"Hi Bud," Ann greeted.

Marie smiled and exclaimed, "Good morning!"

"AA---nn---Muh---ree---fre---en---den," Bud said.

They continued their ride with Bud walking beside. "We came to see how your goats are doing," Ann explained.

Bud responded, "AA---nn---Muh---ree---ha---lp---goo—ttt---fre---en—den."

As they came to the north gate, they spotted the goats leisurely drinking from the small pond. Everything seemed quiet as Ann and Marie got off their horses, tying them to the fence, while Bud opened the gate.

Suddenly, barking could be heard on the south side of the field. It was the pack. All three dogs came running full speed from the tree line toward the goats.

Ann yelled, "It's the dogs! The goats started running in every direction. Marie tried to find a stick, rock or anything to throw. Ann ran toward them screaming and yelling trying to scare them off. Bud froze.

Paying no attention to Ann's scare tactics, the dogs attacked. Two dogs jumped one goat. Ann grabbed a tree branch and started hitting, while yelling at the top of her lungs. Once tasting and smelling blood, they wouldn't let go!

Ann yelled, "Marie, get on your horse, run home and bring pa. We need help!" Marie was scared and started to cry. She screamed, "Ok." Jumping on Red, she kicked him out, yelling, "Let's go!" Red was fast and he liked running to the barn.

All three dogs were on one goat dragging her into the pond. Ann went in after them. "No! No!" She screamed grabbing one dog's tail pulling him off the goat and out of the pond. Bud found rocks and started hitting the dog that had the goat's back leg in his mouth. They landed hard, he yelped and ran with the other dog toward the woods.

The pond was shallow, so Ann could walk on the bottom. She got around to the third dog's head. He had hold of the goat's neck. Just as Bud grabbed his tail, Ann grabbed his head. "Pull hard Bud!" Ann screamed, "Stop! Stop!" As both pulled as hard as they could, the dog let go.

They pulled him off the goat and out of the pond, then let him go. Bud picked up rocks hurling them at him, while Ann begin hitting him with the stick, yelling the entire time. "Get out of here!" She screamed running after him, chasing him toward the woods where the other dogs had gone.

Ann ran back to the pond to help the hurt goat. She was alive, but bobbing up and down in the water about to drown, while rapidly losing blood.

"Help me Bud." He jumped in to help. "Grab her back legs and lift her up. I'll get her head and front legs." Working together they got her out and moved her to a shaded area. "Look, she has a deep hole in her neck. Bud, do you have a hanky?"

"Hay---ke---den," Bud pulled out his hanky and handed it to Ann. She pressed down hard on the hole trying to stop the bleeding.

Just then they heard the pickup coming around the corner. "It's papa and Marie!" Ann was relieved.

"Papa!" Waving her arms, Ann yelled, "Papa, we're over here."

"We're coming," Papa yelled.

They ran to were Bud and Ann had the goat lying in the shade.

"We were able to slow the bleeding," Ann explained. "She may live. Those dogs ran into the woods over there." Ann pointed to the tree line on the south side of the pasture. "You may still be able to find them."

"Ann, I'm gonna borrow your horse." Abe went to his truck and got his gun. "They've probably not gone far. If we don't get rid of them now, they'll keep killing." He got on Jinx. "Once a pack kills, they never stop. Sometimes they even start attacking humans."

"Go papa. We're ok," she assured him. "Bud and Marie can help with the goat. You go. We can load her in the pickup. Please be careful." She began to cry as her papa kicked Jinx into a run to hunt down the predators.

***

Abe knew he must get rid of the dogs. Once getting a taste of blood, killing becomes a sport. He had no drawback from killing the killers. He hoped and prayed they would not get too far away.

He slowed Jinx down to a walk, looking for signs. As he rounded a large pile of rocks leading to the creek bank, he could see a trail of water that had dripped off them after being in the pond.

Abe stopped, tied his horse and took out his gun. Quietly, he walked around the pile of rocks. There in the middle of the running creek water stood the pack, thirsty after their violent attack.

He took aim in the direction of the two dogs standing side by side. His first shot must be perfect, so he could get the other two before they had time to run away. He prayed, "Dear God, these animals are murderers. Please help my aim."

He fired. Two dogs lay dead! They were close enough that one bullet killed both. The other dog took off. Abe quickly cocked and fired again, killing the third and final predator.

Looking up, Abe gave thanks out loud, "Thank you, God, for your help in this endeavor."

***

Ann, Marie and Bud were standing by the pickup as Abe road out of the woods. They ran toward him yelling and waving. He kicked Jinx into a full run. As he reached them, he smiled and exclaimed, "They're gone. Now we're safe and the goats are safe." Marie and Ann hugged their pa.

Bud held out his hand. He smiled his ear-to-ear grin, as he practically shook Abe's arm off. "A---bah---Ba---duh--- fe---rrr---de---den.

Bud and Pastor Abe loaded the doe into the pickup and headed to Ada's barn. Ada was one of the best animal caregivers in the county.

The girls, riding Jinx double, headed home.

Ann was wet and had blood on her clothes, but she didn't care. Just so the goat lived and the dogs were gone for good. She felt like David facing Goliath. With God though, she had strength to face any challenge, even a pack of mean dogs.

Marie felt great because she had done her part, overcoming fear and ridding fast to get help from her pa. Because she asked God for help, she had been able to help everyone; Ann, Bud, the goats, her pa and, ultimately, the community.

***

Bud couldn't read this quote from the Bible *(Proverbs 27:23-27 – NIV)*, but he knew it in his heart, because his Father put it there:

> *Be sure you know the condition of your flocks,*
> *give careful attention to your herds...*
> *When the hay is removed and new growth appears*
> *and the grass from the hills is gathered in,*
> *the lambs will provide you with clothing,*
> *and the goats with the price of a field.*
> *You will have plenty of goats' milk to feed your family...*

CHAPTER ELEVEN

- BUD AT WORK -

Do to others as you would have them do to you.
~ *Luke 6:31 (NIV)* ~

Bud grew into a man. In his own unique way, he became an adult. He decided he needed a job, because he saw that most adults worked. He also started speaking first, instead of just repeating what someone else just said.

He told Mrs. Hodge, "Ba---dua---joh---buh---ma---ke---muh---nee---den. *(Bud job make money.)*

She was surprised. "Ok Bud, you are plenty capable of havin' a job. But in Zafra, there aren't many jobs available. Let me think on it."

Mrs. Hodge had an idea. She decided to run it by Pastor Abe. "Hello Abe, this is Mrs. Hodge."

"Hi Mrs. Hodge. Good to hear from you. How can I help?"

"Abe, I just wanted to run something by you concerning Bud. He is wanting to get a job. I was shocked when he brought this up. I've been thinkin' and have come up with the idea of him sellin' the "Grit." He can be the newspaper delivery man for our area." She gave a nervous laugh, wondering if Abe would agree.

"A great idea Mrs. Hodge. 'Grit' is a great paper, not expensive and Bud likes to walk. I'm sure the community and church family will embrace Bud's endeavor and help him out by purchasing a subscription."

'Grit' is a rural, grassroots paper that is made up of national stories, ads of all kinds and a catalogue section to order anything from buttons to farm equipment. The paper would come once a month and at the individual cost of $1. 50.

With Mrs. Hodge and Pastor Abe's help, Bud started to work. Most everyone in Zafra bought a subscription.

South of Zafra, the Brushy Ridge community had families who knew Bud and wanted to buy the paper. Brushy Ridge was approximately 10 miles through the woods from Zafra.

More often than not, people forgot Bud was coming, because his delivery days would change. There would be a sudden knock at the door and Bud would be standing there, paper in hand, grinning ear-to-ear.

Because Bud usually smelled like goat, his papers sold fast. Everyone wanted to pay him as quickly as possible, so he would be on his way. If they didn't, Bud would just stand there until they came up with the $1.50.

Bud's communication skills may not have been perfect, but he always got his point across. "Gri---tuh---dah---ler---fff---te---den *("Grit"* *$1.50),*" he would say, then open his hand and wait until the money dropped in. It was interesting that even with having limited math skills, he could count the money and give change. His thank you was never spoken; it was his ear-to-ear grin.

If he happened to arrive at meal time, he invited himself to eat. If he ate with the customer one time, he'd try to show up the next time hoping to be just in time for dinner.

Bud's paper route was bringing him in a small salary. He was excited. On Sunday he would stick out his handful of money and say, "Pass---ter---Ab---buh---muh---nee---den---fo---rr---Buh---dah---den."

"Good job Bud. This will help you pay for your goat feed, and give a tithe." Pastor Abe felt it was important to teach Bud how he could help pay his bills and learn to tithe.

"Hel---pah---pa---y---bil---sss---aan---duh---tii---thuh---den."

***

Because Bud walked everywhere, he was vulnerable to predators. Not so much the four-legged kind, but the two-legged kind who were mean and vicious.

One delivery day around 4:00 pm, he was walking down the main Zafra road finishing his route. Around that same time, workers were getting home from their jobs.

Bud happened to be at the turn toward the Hopper farm when Derk and Ted were dropped off at the roads leading to their home.

Lighting up their cigarettes, they spotted Bud walking done the main road. Pointing Derk said, "Hey Ted, let's go have some fun. Looks like he's sellin' papers today. We might get a little cash from 'em." Derk still couldn't pass up a chance to harass Bud, even though he was way passed the age of knowing better.

Ted was glad to help. "Yeah, this ain't gonna be hard. I could use me more cigarette money."

Seeing them coming toward him, Bud knew they were coming to make trouble. There wasn't any need to run, he had tried running many times before. It never worked.

"Hey Bud, what's yah doin'?" Derk started with his tantalizing remarks. "What's that yuh got in you'rn big sack? We might want tuh see." He jerked the sack from Bud.

Ted pushed Bud hard causing him to step backwards. "Yeah, we heard you're the paper boy. We jest might wanta buy one. So---let's see them there papers."

"Paa---per---Gr---it---uh---dah---ler---fff---tee---cc---ee---sss---den." He pointed to his sack.

65

Derk reached in grabbing the paper and opening it. Then he held it up tearing off part of it and handing it to Ted. "Look here, yuh can see this here papers three weeks late. Ain't the letters small? Why I can't even read this."

"Yeah," Ted started ripping up the paper. "This news is old; we already knowed this stuff. Why'd yuh even ask us tuh buy an old paper? This ain't worth nothin' but outhouse paper. You ain't very nice tryin' tuh cheat us."

"Bud, since you're a cheater, we'll just take you'rn money and give it back to everyone who bought this here old paper. So's---let's see. Here it is in the bottom of this bag." Derk reached to the bottom of the sack where Bud kept his money.

"Mm---i---Gr---it---mo---nee---den." Bud reached out trying to take the money from Derk. Ted grabbed Bud's arms, while Derk ripped his shoulder bag and dumped the papers.

"Uhh---uhh---no---uh---den!" Bud yelled like a wild animal caught in a trap.

"Yuh know Bud, we'll be givin' this money back to everybody you's took it from. So's don't go tellin' we stole it or we'll be back to teach yah a lesson. Yuh know what that would mean. We don't take kindly to liars."

Ted pushed Bud hard, he landed with his face in the dirt in the middle of the torn "Grits." Derk kicked him in the side. Bud cried out, "Sss---to---ppp---den!"

Derk and Ted walked off laughing, as they lit up.

Bud lay in the road in the middle of his torn and dirty "Grits." He slowly got up, dusted himself off and begin picking up his ruined papers, putting them into the torn shoulder bag. He was crying, hurt and bleeding.

He had walked about a mile when Pastor Abe came driving down the road. Pastor Abe noticed it was Bud. He was hunched over, hobbling as he walked. Something was wrong!

Stopping the car, he quickly got out. "Bud, are you hurt?" Immediately he saw Bud's bloody dust covered face, the torn "Grits," and he was holding his side.

"What happened Bud?" Bud just looked up as though he was stunned, not answering. "Who did this to you? Derk was one of them, wasn't he?"

"Der---kuh---Ted---duh---too---kkk---mon---nee---torr---"Gr---it"---den. He cried from the pain as he tried to explain what had happened.

Abe was furious! He exclaimed, "Why, Lord, are they always after Bud?"

"Don't you worry one bit. I'll take care of this Bud. Let me help you into the truck." With Pastor Abe's help, Bud slowly climbed in.

Pastor Abe didn't waste any time; he headed straight for Derk's.

As he pulled into the front yard, he barely stopped before opening the door. "Bud you wait here 'til I call for you. I'm gonna talk to Derk's pa."

Seeing Pastor Abe's pickup, Derk's pa came out on the porch.

"Hi there pastor. How 'er yuh? Can I help yah?" He could tell this wasn't a "come to church" visit. "I'm here to talk to Derk. Is he in the house?"

"Yeah, just got home." He could tell how upset Abe was by this red face and the tone of his voice. "Hey Derk," he yelled. "Come out here. Pastor Abe come tuh see yuh."

It took Derk a little time to come out on the porch. Finally, the screen door opened, Derk sheepishly stepped out, his head hanging down.

Pastor Abe stepped on the porch, stopping directly in front of Derk's face. "Derk, I found Bud walking down the road heading home and stopped to pick him up. He was crying and hurt, with dirt and blood on him, holding his side where he was kicked--probably has a broken rib. He said you and Ted knocked him down, stealing his paper route money."

Turning toward his pickup, Abe yelled, "Come here Bud!" Bud slowly got out, holding his side and limping, he walked cautiously toward the porch.

Derk's pa could see the dirt and blood on Bud's face and shirt. His face also got red. He yelled, "Derk, did yuh have anything tuh do with this 'ere meanness? You better tell the truth or the punishment 'ill get worse."

Derk put his head down and mumbled, "Yah."

"Look at me boy when you'rn speakin' tuh me; speak up!" He shouted.

He looked up, "It was Ted's idea." Derk immediately blamed his buddy.

Through clenched teeth his pa continued, "Where's the paper route money? Get it now, and give it back to Bud!"

"Ted and I split it." He reached in his pocket and brought out $3.

"This is all I have. Ted's got the other $3." He kept his eyes down while handing the money to Pastor Abe.

With clenched teeth, Pastor Abe exploded, "If this ever happens again, I will bring in the law. Do you understand? It's time for this to STOP!"

"Yes sir." Derk kept his head down.

Derk's pa grabbed his arm and pushed him toward the barn. "You get to the barn---NOW!"

Pastor Abe helped Bud back into the truck. As they drove away, they could hear Derk yelling how he didn't do anything. "It was all Ted!"

Their next visit was to Ted's house. When they got there, the same scene took place. Except Pastor Abe told Ted he would be sending the law over, because he had physically abused Bud.

Ted confessed and gave up the $3. Just like his buddy, he blamed Derk for the whole thing. Both young men were fools. They were both old enough to know better.

***

As Pastor Abe drove Bud home. He had a talk with him, "Bud, if they get hold of you again, you could be badly hurt. Now Derk and Ted will blame you for their being caught, punished and again in trouble with the law."

"From now on, deliver your papers earlier in the day. Ok Bud? Do you understand?"

"Un---der---sta---n---dd---den." Even though it hurt his mouth, Bud tried to smile his ear-to-ear grin. Always his way of saying thanks.

***

Until the day he died, Bud continued selling 'Grit'. It was a joy to see his smile and get his paper. Even though sometimes he smelled like his goats, timed it just right to eat a meal with his clients and the news was three weeks late, everyone looked forward to Bud's visit. Because it was...well...Bud.

Wisdom says, "Do not say, 'I'll pay you back for this wrong!' Wait for the Lord and he will avenge you." Bud always waited, and the Lord kept His promise.

CHAPTER TWELVE

- COMMUNION - CALENDARS -
CHURCH-WORK -

*Whatever the Lord pleases, He does, in heaven
and in earth, in the sea and in all the deeps.*
~ Psalm 135:6 (NASB) ~

Bud continued to become more of an adult. Over time, even with his limited speech and mental capacity, he came to realize he was no longer a child. Bud learned by watching how adults had responsibilities and he was their age. Bud was growing older and he wanted to do his part.

Taking his Bible to church was a habit he acquired from the time he was a young boy, but now he wanted help finding the chapter and verses.

"A---nn---fri---en---duh---den." Not asking, Bud laid his Bible in Ann's lap.

"Sure Bud. Watch." She turned to the book of Matthew. "Matthew is in the New Testament."

Bud repeated, "Nuu---tess---tuh---ment---den." He wanted to learn. But he didn't stop there. Bud saw there were many other ways to serve.

***

Every Sunday, Zafra Church observed the communion service. One Sunday after a week of extreme rain, water was over the bridges and many members couldn't get through to attend church.

Of course, Bud was there. Come rain or shine Bud never missed a service.

Low on men, Pastor Abe saw he didn't have enough to serve communion. So, he asked Bud. "Bud would you help serve communion today." "Ba---ud---ser---ve---cah---mun---ion---den."

When communion time came, Bud jumped up and pretty much ran to help. Before services, Pastor Abe told Billy to help Bud, if he needed, because it was his first time.

As they rounded the pews to serve, to everyone's amazement, Bud knew exactly what to do. All these years he had been watching and learning how communion was served.

After Bud's first time serving, it was a done deal. Bud wanted to serve every Sunday. Pastor Abe tried to explain. "Bud, I will tell you when it's your time to serve. It's important for all the men to take turns."

Bud smiled and proudly said, "Buh---da---serr---ve---den."

If pastor Abe forgot to tell Bud he wasn't serving, he would hurry to the table even if the correct number of servers were already there. If he ever got to the table, he wouldn't sit down. One of the other servers had to relinquish their position.

Bud believed he was doing a great service for the church. It was something to watch as he served. He bent low to pick up the bread or the juice tray, walking slowly as he passed them. It was as though he thought he was literally in the presence of Jesus serving the last supper.

Often times, some of the men serving approached communion like a drill. Not an ounce of emotion expressing the fact Jesus' precious blood spilled and His body broken for each of them.

Watching Bud serve communion brought meaning and life to the sacrament. It was as though Bud envisioned standing at the foot of Jesus' cross.

No person told Bud nor explained to him how he should act when he served. It was apparent the Spirit taught him.

Pastor Abe gave up trying to have Bud take turns. No one every complained.

***

Another sign of Bud's growing into adult life was his gathering of "things." He started wanting items he saw grown-ups use.

The first items on his "things" list were calendars; not calendar, but calendars! He began asking everyone for calendars. The only problem; whoever gave him the calendar was automatically expected to get him one every year.

Bud's fetish for calendars was not wasted. He used them in his kitchen for wall décor. Also, he kept his personal calendar in the kitchen. Every day he marked off the day with a checkmark. Only one thing was different, on Sunday he marked it off with a cross. No one ever told Bud to do this. It came naturally.

Curious, Pastor Abe asked, "Bud, why do you have the picture of a cross on Sundays. Without hesitation Bud explained, "Ccc---rro---sss---Jee---uss---frr—end---den."

***

One Sunday, Bud showed up at church with a calendar and ask Kerri for help to learn to find the date. "Bu---d---lea---rn---to---rre---ad---den." He pointed to the open calendar. "Wh---ah---tuh---da---y---den?"

"After church we will help you learn. Ok?"

Bud agreed, "Ok---den."

After church Bud met with Kerri. "Ok, Bud, let me show you. At the top you see the days. Repeat them after me: Sunday, ..." Sticking out his lips, Bud repeated, "Suh---da---den." Slowly, they went through each day of the week.

"Now look underneath the days of the week. You see this number. This is the date. Now you know the date and the day of each month. Every month has up to thirty or thirty-one days, and when the new month comes, the numbers start over."

"Let's play a game. I'll call out the day and the number and you see if you can find it."

Bud smiled his grin and replied, "Ga---me---den."   .

"Wednesday, January 22nd." Bud searched till he recognized Wednesday. Putting his finger there he scrolled down to the twenty-second. He exclaimed, "Hee---rr---den!" Kerri clapped and praised him for his accomplishment. Bud was understanding how it worked.

Mama Wilson and Mrs. Elder would be so happy to know their teaching Bud the alphabet and numbers was not in vain. At the age of forty-five Bud was beginning to understand letters and recognize numbers.

***

Another grown up item Bud wanted was a radio. He loved music and he noticed radios and televisions were in most adults' cars and houses.

One day Bud was visiting Pastor Abe's family and their radio was on. Bud went over to the radio and put his hand on it, "Baa---dah---wa---nts---rai---dee---oh---den.

Kerri immediately saw his smile. "You want a radio?"

"Ye---ss---den."   .

"It cost about $20 Bud. Do you have money?" Kerri asked.

"Mon---nee---at---uh---ho----mee---den." He headed toward the door to go home and get his money.

Kerri stopped him. "Bud, you don't need to go get the money now, we can get it Sunday when we pick you up for Church. We won't go to town till after Sunday."

"O----k-k-k---den." He kept walking heading out the door and down the hill.

73

Watching him walk down the hill, Ann asked, "Mama did he understand you?"

"I'm sure he did. He probably just needed to get home. These days Bud has his own way."

He didn't understand her. In about an hour, Bud showed back up with a small sack of savings.

"Mon---nee---foo---rr---rai---dee---oh---den." He handed Kerri the sack.

"We'll count your money and see if you have twenty dollars. Here Ann count his money." She poured out his savings on the table.

"Gr---it---mon---nee---den," Bud happily explained.

As she began to count, Marie came into the kitchen and handed a dollar to Ann. "Mama, I want to help Bud. Here's a dollar to go with his savings."

Ann ran to her room and came back with two dollars. "Being alone and all, Bud really needs the radio." Ann was happy to give what she had.

Kerri and Abe had raised their children to be faithful in their giving. Kerri was pleased her daughters showed their faith by blessing Bud. "Girls, God's gonna shower His blessings on you. Because you can't out give Him."

When Ann finished counting, she happily announced, "Bud you have a total of eighteen dollars and thirty-five cents. With the three-dollar donation your total is twenty-one dollars and thirty-five cents."

Kerri held up Bud's sack of money. "Bud when we go to town, we can get the radio." He reached out to shake Marie's and Ann's hand, his hard and long handshake, smiling his "thank you" ear-to-ear grin.

On Tuesday, Pastor Abe bought the radio. With tax added, the amount came to twenty-one dollars and thirty-five cents. When faith is involved, God always comes through with the right amount of blessing.

Bud loved his radio. He always played it so loud the music could be heard from his living room all the way out to the main road.

***

Soon after the radio had been bought, the Zafra community was plagued with a thief. When a family was gone the thief would invade the home. Everyone knew he was from the community because he knew when families were gone.

Usually small items were stolen: guns, tools, televisions, radios, etc. When Bud heard about the thief, he decided to hide his radio.

Abe went to visit Bud to see if he had become a victim. When he arrived, Bud insisted upon him coming inside his house to show where he had hidden his radio from the thief.

Leading Abe into his bedroom, he said, "Hi---dd---rai---dee---oh---den." He pointed to his chest of drawers where he had put the radio in one drawer, then had turned the entire chest backwards so the front was up against the wall.

Pastor Abe laughed till tears came into his eyes. "Good job, Bud. You're a smart man. No thief will find your hiding place."

"Goo---dah---jo---ba---den!" Bud repeated, then he smiled his ear-to-ear grin and joined in the laughter.

***

As the years went by, Bud participated in more adult service for the Church. Leading the congregation in prayer became important to him. Because of his speech, he had never been asked to pray during a worship service. The first time he prayed out loud came as a complete surprise.

One Sunday Bud went forward to serve at the Lord's Table. Except this time, he took a different position. He stood where the person who prayed for the cup stood.

Brother Turner had been designated to pray for the cup, and when Bud took his spot, he didn't know what to do. To push Bud out of the way wasn't an option. Instead of making a scene, he took Bud's place to serve.

Pastor Abe started to tell Bud to move. Then he prayed. "God he is Your child, you decide what is best."

Instead of the congregation bowing their heads and shutting their eyes for the communion prayer, everyone's eyes were on Bud.

Bud bowed his head, squinched his eyes tight and begin. "Loh---rr---duh---pra—y—fo---r---cu---ppp---of---Jee---sss---den." That was it---the perfect prayer!

Bud's words came out as clear as a bell. Bud knew he was to pray for the cup that held the juice representing our Lord's precious blood. No one told Bud what to pray, but he knew from watching and learning. And of course, the Spirit's intercession.

After services, the old gang got together and cornered Bud. Ted started the conversation, "Hey Bud. You wasn't supposed tuh pray. You know'd you can't say nothin' plain. Nobody can understand yuh. What is 'Loh---r---d---cuh---uh---uh…den, ha ha.'" He mimicked Bud. Derk, Marilyn and the rest joined in the stutter.

Marilyn leaned into Bud's face. "Jee—sss", she mockingly stammered. "Mar---rrr---lee---nnn."

"Den," Derk howled, "Don't ferget the 'den' on the end. Oh, I made a rhyme, 'den' on the end." The entire group spit out their ugliness.

Brother Turner heard the hateful laughter and extra loud talk. Wondering what was going on, he went around the corner to see. Surrounding Bud were the harassers.

Brother Turner could not believe they continued to be hateful. He was stunned at how the now old gang, never quit. As the saying goes, "There's no fool like an old fool."

"What do you think you're doing? All of you leave Bud alone," Brother Turner hollered!

They all turned hurrying away, because they saw Pastor Abe coming around the corner. Some even had their heads down, showing a little shame for once.

Brother Turner put his hand on Bud's shoulder. "Bud don't let these idiots bother you."

Bud tried to smile, but it seemed to be stunted. The harassment hurt.

Brother Turner explained to Pastor Abe what had happened. "I'll take Bud home and make sure he's ok."

"I don't know what to say," Pastor Abe shook his head. "No matter what their age, they enjoy harassing Bud. It's as Proverbs 21:24 (NIV) says: 'The proud and arrogant person---'Mocker' is his name---behaves with insolent fury.' A perfect picture of this group."

These fools never ceased to harass Bud, nor anyone else vulnerable to their meanness. Age never changed them. Their persecution, intimidation and cruelty continued to move right along with them.

Bud, listened to the wisdom of God speaking to him from scripture:

> *Be sure of this: the wicked will not go unpunished, but those who are righteous will go free. (Proverbs 11:21- NIV)*

***

Bud continued to grow and be involved in his church work.

Every year the mountain area churches would get together for a tent revival. These meetings would last at least a week, with Bud never missing a night.

One of the fun events at these meetings was the special music. Every night different churches would be assigned the job of bringing a group to sing.

The night Zafra Church was performing, Bud decided it was time for him to bring special music. But, of course, no one knew!

Pastor Abe introduced the group, "We are so glad to be here representing our Zafra congregation. We hope you all enjoy our songs of praise."

Everyone enjoyed the singing. The performance was followed by a huge round of applause and "Amens." As the group started to sit down, Bud jumps up and runs on the stage to the piano, sits down, places his hands on the keys and begins hitting the keys up and down the piano with both hands. He moved back and forth while singing:

Fing---loh---swee---tuh---cher---ree—aut
(Swing low, sweet chariot)

Cuh---men---fer---tuh---ca---ree---me---hoh---mah
(Comin' for to carry me home)

Fing---loh---swee---tuh---cher---ree---aut
(Swing low, sweet chariot)

Cuh---men---fer ---tuh---ca---ree---me---hoh---mah
(Comin' for to carry me home)

Finished, he stood up, looked at everyone, smiled his ear-to-ear grin and marched to his seat.

For a second everyone sat stunned. There was not a sound. Then Ann started to clap, then another until the entire audience rose to their feet. Amongst the clapping were shouts of praise. Bud smiled his great big ear-to-ear grin. His first solo was a hit.

***

Yes, Bud became an adult. As Samuel in the Bible grew up as a servant in God's house, Bud also grew up with a mind of a five-year-old, as a servant in God's house.

***

Years ago, the psalmist stated, *"Surely goodness and mercy shall follow me all the days of my life, and I will dwell in the house of the Lord forever." (Psalm 23:6 – NKJV)*

He must have known Bud. Bud was simply a five-year-old with an adult body who had goodness and mercy following him all the days of his life. He dwelled in the house of the Lord from time into eternity.

CHAPTER THIRTEEN

- RECAPITULATION -

The grass withers, the flower fades... But the word of our God stands forever.
~ *Isaiah 40:6-8 (NASB)* ~

"God...seems to do nothing Himself which He can possibly delegate to His creatures." Through Bud, God shared His love, fellowship, kindness and grace. Bud's life exemplified what Jesus prayed, *"Thy kingdom come, Thy will be done, on Earth as it is in Heaven." (Matthew 6:9 ESV)*

***

Bud was now in his 60's. He continued serving the church, selling 'Grit', tending his goats and being a friend to the Zafra community.

Those bullies who hounded Bud were getting older. Yet whenever the opportunity presented itself, they still made Bud their jester, mimicking his speech, mocking his mannerisms, taunting him about why he never married, with sexual innuendos.

God continues to allow them to reap the repercussions of their actions. He warned them---"You will reap what you sow." Their lives were and still are full of trouble and despair. They never came to realize rebellion is the devil's wheelhouse and they are his pawns.

God keeps His promises: "The wicked are overthrown and are no more." or "Be sure of this: "The wicked will not go unpunished."

On the other hand, Bud obeyed God's promise: "Do not say, 'I'll pay you back for this wrong!' Wait for the Lord and He will avenge you!"

Bud won!

***

At about the age of 63, Bud started to have health issues. In the early part of his final few years, he developed chronic colds. Pastor Abe and Kerri encouraged him to stay home when he felt sick, or had a fever.

No matter what the weather, or how he felt, Bud did not heed their warning.

"Hi Bud." He was selling 'Grit's'. Kerri stopped the car to speak with him.

"Ker---rie---den!" Bud smiled his ear-to-ear grin.

Immediately Kerri saw beads of sweat falling into his eyes. "Bud, are you ok? You're sweating and you look pale. Please get into the car and I'll drive you home."

He got in. Kerri put her hand on his forehead, it was hot. "You have a high fever. We're going to get you to the doctor."

"'Gr---it'---den," holding up the papers letting her know he hadn't finished his deliveries.

"Tomorrow I can finish delivering your paper," she assured him.

"Ooh---kk---den---Buh---duh---sic---kk---den."

Over the next few years, Bud had several of these episodes. Pastor Abe, Kerri and the church family carefully watched after him.

***

Many changes took place during these last years of Bud's life. Those he was close to passed away. Preston, who found Bud when he was lost, Daisey, Thelma Lou, Bertha, and Mrs. Shepherd, women in the church who loved Bud and helped take care of him, went home to be with the Lord.

Ada turned 83 and moved to another state to live with her daughter. Her son Bobby had married and moved away.

Bud's care giver Mrs. Hodge, came to give her life to Jesus. Bud influenced her more than she influenced him. Her language even changed. Instead of using "Jesus" as a derogatory adjective, she used His name in prayer. She went home to be with the Lord six months after her one hundredth birthday! Her daughter Johnnie, continued as Bud's caregiver.

***

In his last years, Bud changed in many ways. The most interesting thing was he began to write. Every week he brought hand-written notes to people in the church family. He would take the note to the person he had written it for, then stand there until they read it.

"Aa----nn---Buh---duh---wri---tuh---no----te---den." He handed it to her.

"Thank you, Bud." She opened it, and read:

BUDFRIENDKERRIWARDFRIENDABECHRISTMASDECEMBER22ANN

Bud wrote in all caps with no spaces between the words. "Thank you, Bud. This is really good. You're so kind. I'm also excited about the Christmas program. You will make a great shepherd and your baby goats will be perfect for the manger scene. I can't wait!" She gave him a hug,

"I'll read your note to Mama and Papa. They'll be excited you thought of them."

Bud gave his ear-to-ear grin "Buh---da---bri---ng---mo---re---no---te --- den."

Bud kept writing. The notes became Bud's new communication skill.

On Sunday Bud brought a strange note to pastor Abe. "Why thank you Bud." Bud stood there till he read it:

LOSTTHREEFRIENDSBUD
LOSTFOLKWILSONFAMILYDEATH

"Yes Bud, you have lost some of your friends, and your family. But remember 'The Lord gives and He takes away.' This is what His Word says. Someday we all will be taken to be with Jesus in heaven."

"Buh---da---se---e---fri---end---haa---ven---den."

"Yes, you will be there some day with the Lord and all of your church friends and family." Pastor Abe felt uneasy about Bud's conversation about dying.

Kerri was curious, "Bud who is helping you write your notes? You are doing such a great job."

"Joh---nie---den."

"Bud, why don't you ask Johnnie to come to church with you? She came all the time when she was in school, but she hasn't been here in several years."

"Buh---da---as---kuh---Joh---nie---too---chur---ch---den." Shaking his head as he spoke.

Bud did ask Johnnie and she started coming. Not long after her return, during an invitation, Johnnie walked down the aisle to give her life to Jesus. She was baptized in the Zafra Church Cow Creek baptistry. Bud was ecstatic. "Jes---us---sa---vuh---Joh---nnie---den."

"Yes, Bud, you helped her by inviting her to church. You're a witness for the Lord." Pastor Abe shook Bud's hand.

Bud's life was lived for the Shepherd. Without ever knowing, Bud had a part in many accepting Christ as Savior and Lord. Bud begin to understand what it meant to be a witness.

***

Physically, Bud begin to show his age. His shoulders drooped and his hair became gray. His spiritual health grew, while his physical heath diminished, though he never complained. God sustained him.

***

Bud was turning 70. The Zafra Church always celebrated Bud's birthday with a cake and dinner on the ground. This year Ann was determined to make it a celebration of a lifetime.

Everyone was on board with food and decorations. The celebration would be more than just a birthday party; It would be an appreciation of Bud's lifelong loving kindness shown to his church and community.

Because it was such a very special birthday, Ann felt it warranted him a very special gift. "Papa, for Bud's birthday I'm getting him a new suit with all the extras, even shoes." Ann waited for his reaction. He smiled, "What a perfect idea. Your Mama and I are all in. We'll donate to the cause."

Since Bud was around 30 years old, he wore a suit every Sunday. Although the jackets and paints didn't match most of the time, and his ties were hand-me-downs, Bud wanted to dress like an adult.

Ann was newly married to Adam and they didn't have a lot of money to spend. "Adam, for Bud's birthday we're getting him a suit with all the extras. I know it will be expensive for us, but Papa said he and Mama would help."

Adam smiled, "That's a great idea, let's do it!"

Ann bought Bud a beautiful smoky gray suit, white shirt and a silver tie. She also bought new black dress shoes. Ann was excited. No one more than Bud deserved such a great gift. She prayed, "Lord thank you for Bud. Thank you for allowing him to be in my life and to teach me about faith in action."

After the purchase, Ann went straight to Bud's house. When he came to the door he didn't look very well. "Buh---da---see---kk---uh---den." He stammered with little energy.

"I have something that will cheer you up," she said going into his house. She opened up the sack and pulled out all the items, laying them on his bed. Bud went from no smile to his usual ear-to-ear grin.

"New---sho---sss---den." Bud's eyes got big as he pulled out the shoes. Immediately he tried them on.

She held each item up as she spoke, "Yes, a suit, shirt, tie and socks. Now, you can't wear these 'til Sunday morning. Remember, Sunday is church picture day, and that's when you wear your new clothes and shoes." She told him this to keep his birthday celebration a surprise.

Bud nodded and replied, "Pic---tur---daa---den."

"Yes, Bud. I will be coming to pick you up for church and help you with your tie. Ok?"

"O---kkk---den."

The new clothes cheered him up. Before Ann left, he gave her his big ear-to-ear grin.

***

Sunday Ann arrived at Buds early. He felt better and was his usually smiling self. She helped him with his tie, even combing his hair. Bud grabbed his Bible as they headed for church.

It was a beautiful day. It seemed as though the Lord had made the sky clearer and the sun brighter just for Bud's birthday celebration.

Over two hundred of Bud's friends and church family covered the grounds. When everyone joined in singing *Happy Birthday*, Bud realized the celebration was for him. "Look at this crowd, Bud" Pastor Abe pointed out. "See how you are loved. Your entire family is here for your celebration.

"Buh---da---lo—veh---th---em---den." His ear-to-ear grin stuck in place for the day.

The meal was extra special with all of Bud's favorite dishes. He took pictures with the Church family, his family and with Pastor Abe's family. He received multitudes of gifts. To end the celebration everyone held up a helium balloon and at the same time let it go up to the heavens with a prayer for Bud.

No one knew another celebration for Bud was about to take place.

***

Two years after his Birthday celebration on Sunday morning, Pastor Abe went to pick Bud up for church. When he drove up, Bud was not on the porch Bible in hand waiting for his ride. Abe honked the horn, waited, but still no Bud. Something was wrong.

Abe went to the door. Opening the door, he yelled "Bud!" He heard a very weak feeble answer, "Hee---rr---den." Quickly Abe moved into his bedroom. He was in bed very sick, his breathing labored, white as a sheet, sweat pouring down his face. Yet he had a stack of blankets covering him and his sock cap on because he was shivering.

"Bud, how long have you been sick?" He could barely be heard, "Tuh—oo---daa---ee—den."

Abe felt his face. It was scorching! There was no thermometer to be found. "Bud, I'll wash your face with cool water. You have high fever." Bud never responded. He just laid there with his eye's closed, breathing hard.

Finding a washcloth, Abe wiped Bud's face with cool water while getting him a glass full to drink. He got a glass of water. "Bud, you must drink this. You're very hot."

Bud started trying to get up. "Bud don't move! Lie still. As soon as you drink all the water, I'll get you dressed. We're going to the emergency room.

"No---oh---den!" Bud yelled. His face red and eyes full of fear. Pastor Abe had never seen Bud afraid of anything.

"Bud you're going to the doctor. You're very sick. Stay in bed." Pastor Abe gently pushed him back down. "Lie still Bud. Now drink this water." Pastor Abe got most of the water down him. "I'm going to go get Kerri and a couple of the men from church. I'll be right back. Do not get out of bed! You're very sick. If you try to get out of bed you might pass out."

Bud closed his eyes, not responding.

86

Abe prayed, "Lord please help Bud. He's your child. Help him not to fight us as we get him to the hospital. Thy will be done. In Jesus' name, amen."

***

Abe borrowed a church member's van, then picked up Brother Dave and Adam to help get Bud loaded into the van. Kerri drove their car.

After arriving at the hospital, as the paramedics picked him up, Bud never moved. He was unconscious.

On the way into the ER, he woke up and started making noises as though he was agitated. He kept moving his arms, and tossing his head back and forth. By the time they had him in a room he was fighting, kicking, flinging his arms, and yelling.

"We've got to give him a sedative." One of the Paramedics announced.

Bud kept yelling, "Sto---ah---pp---den!"

A paramedic asked, "Who is his next of kin?"

Pastor Abe shook his head. "He has no family members here. Just do what you need to do. His sisters and brother don't help him, he's on his own. A lady from our church is his caregiver, but she doesn't have 'Power of Attorney'. I 'll sign."

The paramedics wasted no time in getting him strapped down. The sedative began taking effect.

Several church members arrived, as the waiting room grew full. Pastor Abe and Kerri called for a time of prayer.

With his voice shaking, Pastor Abe announced, "Bud is very sick. His fever's high and he's dehydrated. Most likely he's been sick two or three days. Bud is our precious brother. Everyone please join hands and pray what God is putting on our hearts to pray."

As the prayers begin there was not a dry eye in the room. The prayers were for God's will to be done; thankfulness for Bud; comfort and peace for all; and doctors and nurses to find the problem. Just as the prayers finished, the doctor came to the room.

87

"Bud is a very sick man. He is dehydrated and has pneumonia. The fever has probably been around 105 degrees for more than forty-eight hours. His infection is serious, and his age won't help him any. The virus kills seventy-five percent of those over the age of sixty. The next twenty-four hours are crucial. Prayer is your assignment. The Lord's will be done." He turned and walked quickly down the hall.

The church family went to their knees. Many were in tears. Some prayed softly; others prayed together in groups of two or three. Bud was loved. His life had nurtured their growth in grace, realizing how Bud's love was just like Jesus' love...unconditional.

***

When Bud woke up, being in an unfamiliar place made him scared. He started again trying to pull out the wires he was hooked to.

Bud was never hysterical. He was always calm. But not this time. They had to give him another sedative.

Pastor Abe and Kerri stayed at the hospital. The nurse allowed them to alternate being in his room.

***

The next morning Bud woke up when Pastor Abe happened to be in the room. "Hi Bud. How we doing?" He smiled giving Bud a pat.

Bud looked at Abe with a blank stare. "Bu---dh---go-----hoo---mm---den." He started to get up.

"Bud stay here. These doctors and nurses will help you get well. Then you can go home."

"Hoo---mm---den." He started again shaking his arms trying to free himself from the hookups. He moved his head up and down, hitting it hard on the pillow.

Abe sat on the bed close to Bud, gently holding down his arms. "Bud, please do not shake your arms. You'll hurt yourself and the IV might come out. When they try to put it in again it'll hurt!" Bud looked at Abe and begin calming down.

"You're very sick. All of us are praying for you to get well."

"Hoo---mm---den." He never heard Pastor Abe.

Abe slowly moved his hands from holding Bud's arms. He stayed quiet and still.

"We are going to take you home as soon as the doctor says we can. You must rest and do everything he tells you to do. God will protect you, so don't be afraid. As soon as you're well, Kerri and I will take you home and look after you."

Abe knew the story of Bud being lost at the age of five, and the fear he had of everyone, even his own family. Now his fear had returned. He was afraid of all he was going through. He was five again, alone in those dark woods.

"Bud, I will go now so you can rest. Kerri and I will be just outside these doors if you need us. We are not leaving until you can go home." When Bud heard Pastor Abe say he and Kerri were staying, he took a deep breath of relief.

"Hoo---mm---den," he repeated over and over until he finally shut his eyes and slept.

Abe barely made it through the ER doors before he began to cry. He quickly turned, hiding himself behind a door. He didn't want Kerri nor church members seeing him upset. Bud was his faith gage. He had this feeling, and he never went by feelings, Bud would be going home and it wouldn't be to Zafra!

Wiping his eyes, he walked to the waiting room. At the same time, the doctor came in to give an updated report on Bud.

"These people are all Bud's neighbors and church family; you can give the report to all of us." Abe requested.

It was evident the news wasn't much better, "Bud is a very sick man. He has pneumonia, the worst kind. Infection is all through his body. If it had been caught sooner, we could have had a better chance." Bowing his head, he continued, "It's in God's hands We have done everything medically we can do. We're keeping him here for now." Sounds of crying and sobs could be heard. "Do you have any questions?"

No one asked questions; they were praying.

***

For the next twenty-four hours, Kerri and Abe alternated being with Bud. He slept.

Many of the congregation came to the hospital to pray and see if there was anything they could do. Abe and Kerri assured them of God's grace and mercy and how His will is good and perfect.

That evening around 5:00 pm the doctor came back to the waiting room.

"Bud's vital signs are stable. His white cell count is still up from the infection, but his fever is down. He's still on oxygen but his breathing has slowed down. We have kept him sedated because of his trying to jerk out the IVs and get out of bed. If all goes well, tomorrow we'll get him into a private room." He again asks, "Are there any questions?"

"Thank you, doctor." Abe and Kerri said at the same time. Abe continued "We appreciate all you're doing."

Kerri asked, "Do you think he will soon wake up enough for us to talk with him?"

"Not likely. We have him pretty much sedated. He needs the rest and I'm concerned he might hurt one of the nurses with all of his thrashing around. Maybe in the morning." His name was called over the intercom and he left.

Abe pulled Kerri to the side. "Kerri, I don't have a good feeling about Bud's situation. Never have I seen him look like this. And I don't mean his sickness, but his eyes. It's like he's not seeing me. Have you noticed, or am I just imagining things?"

Kerri could see he was upset. She took both of his hands and faced him. "Abe, I feel the same way. All he talks about is 'going home'. It has struck me that he will go home; it may not be to the home in Zafra, but the home prepared by the Shepherd."

Abe took her in his arms; they wept.

***

Noon, the next day, Bud woke up. Immediately he started yelling, "hoo---mm---den." He kept yelling and begin again pulling on his IVs, trying to jerk out everything he was hooked to. The alarm went off.

Abe heard it outside the ICU doors. He headed to Bud's room. "Bud." He kept yelling his name as he ran into his room. "Bud don't, you'll hurt yourself!"

He ran to Bud's bed trying to push him back down. He was acting like a caged animal. "Hoo---mm---den---Go---hoo---mm---den!" Security got him back into bed. This time they strapped him down, giving him another sedative.

Taking Bud's hand, Abe told him, "Bud please don't fight; as soon as you get well, Kerri and I will take you home." Bud held on tight to Abe's hand, "Bu---d---go---hoo---mm---den."

"Bud don't you worry, Kerri and I made you a promise when the doctor releases you, we will take you home."

Bud started to calmed down. He closed his eyes. Suddenly, with his eyes closed he grinned his ear-to-ear grin. As Abe watched, Bud's smile stayed as he drew his last breath.

Bud's prayer was answered; he was home.

***

Kerri and Abe stood by Bud's bedside where his body lay. Both amazed at how his ear-to-ear grin was fixated on his face. However, they understood why it stayed there; Bud was home!

CHAPTER FOURTEEN

- HOME -
...I go to prepare a place for you, I will come
back and take you to be with me that
you also may be where I am.
~ *John 14: 2-3 (NIV)* ~

The Zafra Church planned a "Going Home" celebration for Bud. The day broke clear with a bright blue sky, and not a cloud in sight. A soft breeze gently blew through the tall pines sounding like voices singing. People came from the entire county. Vehicles were parked on the side of the road for more than a mile.

Bud's celebration dinner was a banquet. Table clothes, flowers, and candles covered the tables. In honor of his love for fellowship dinners Bud's favorite dishes were served.

The sanctuary was full an hour before the service. Extra chairs were sat up in the isles and outside the church by the windows for the overflow of guests on both sides of the sanctuary.   All the windows were open for everyone to hear the service.

Kerri begin playing the prelude twenty minutes before the service begin. She played Bud's favorite hymns loud and in his favorite gospel style: "When I See the Blood," "What a Friend We Have in Jesus," "Footsteps of Jesus."   These familiar hymns brought to mind Bud's loud off pitch singing.

The service began with everyone singing, "Power in the Blood."   The force of the singing and powerful lyrics, lifted everyone's spirit.

Pastor Dalton and his wife Ethel came back for Bud's celebration. He gave the invocation. Stepping to the podium looking up, he lifted his hands:

92

Oh Lord, today we come to honor our brother in Christ Ward "Bud" Wilson. We thank you for the opportunity we all have had to be Bud's friends, and brothers and sisters in Christ. Friends are friends forever, if the Lord's the Lord of them.

Bud's homecoming celebration must be shouted from these mountaintops. Everything that has breath is praising you today for his life. The trees clap their hands, and the rocks rejoice. And so, must we rejoice with all creation.

Bud is finally home with you and Jesus!
In our Lord and Savior's precious name
AA---men---den

As pastor Dalton sat down, joyful tears were flowing. Everyone smiled at his ending, and joined in on the "Amen."

Bud was like family to Ada's kids. As he grew up, her son Bobby saw Bud every day when he came to feed his goats. He and Bud became very good friends.

Because of this friendship, Bobby wanted to read Bud's obituary:

Ward 'Bud' Wilson, of Zafra, Oklahoma, passed away on Wednesday evening in Mena, Arkansas. He was born in Clarksville, Texas, to the late Robert and Ura Johnson Wilson. He is survived by three sisters: Nancy May Lloyd, Rosie Alice Willis, and Ura B. Parsons; one brother Albert David Wilson; and numerous nieces and nephews, plus great nieces and great nephews.

It is such an honor to be able to be a part of his "Going Home" celebration, and have the opportunity to speak about this tremendous friend and brother in Christ, Ward 'Bud' Wilson.

He paused for a moment to wipe his eyes, then continued:

God put Bud in this very place for a reason. All of us have our own thoughts of exactly what that reason was, because Bud's life affected all of us in our own personal way. He wasn't rich, handsome, popular, smart, educated---he was just---well---

> *Bud. His character was one of loving kindness pointing to his heavenly Father. Bud never forgot a name or a face, including the faces and names of his goats.*

Everyone reacted with smiles and soft giggles.

Bobby finished by saying:

> *But the greatest name he never forgot was the One he emulated; Jesus Christ the Shepherd. His face is exactly what Bud saw as he took his last walk from the hospital room into his Shepherd's open arms. As he looked up and saw Him there, all the fear subsided, the IVs fell from his arms. Bud was free! Free to speak and not stutter---to be loved and never bullied---to read and write---and, finally, to sing in perfect harmony with the angel choir. Every lyric perfectly clear.*

Everyone clapped as Bobby stepped off the stage.

Pastor Abe stepped to the pulpit and begin the message:

> *Here lies the physical body of a man. A man more whole than most men. A man with only a few physically blood kinfolks; but a host of Spiritually blood kinfolk; never went to college; but had a doctorate in theology; could not speak clearly, but communicated the gospel to anyone around him; had absolutely no money, but in every way was a rich man. Bud's name will never be forgotten---Bud lives!*

Around the room came many voices raising an "Amen" or "Praise God."

Raising his voice another notch, he proclaimed:

> *Bud always had his ear-to-ear grin. His smile was famous; a smile hardly ever leaving his face. When time came for him to go home, his Father took away his fear, putting his ear-to-ear grin in its place. In the blink of an eye, he went home! Kerri and I were standing beside his bed, his face plastered with his ear-to-ear grin permanently in its place!*

Again, everyone clapped, but louder.

He raised his voice and shouted:

> *Death can be a violent rape of life. Death has been described as chilling. What makes death potent is it appears so----final! Bud smiled at death. Bud accepted death as a defeated foe. He could look death straight in the eye and smile. Bud smiled at death because he knew the One who gives us eternal life; Bud smiled at death, because death is swallowed up in victory; Bud smiled at death, because in Christ he would rise---incorruptible---he would be changed. Bud's ear-to-ear grin can't be wiped from his face because---DEATH IS DEAD!*

Everyone went to their feet clapping and shouting an "Amen," "Yes," "Hallelujah" and "Praise God!" The outpouring continued for several minutes!

Ann came forward to lead the congregation in *Amazing Grace*:

> *Amazing grace how sweet the sound,*
> *that saved a wretch like me.*
> *I once was lost but now am found,*
> *was blind but now I see.*
>
> *The Lord has promised good to me;*
> *His Word my hope secures.*
> *His will my shield and portion be*
> *As long as life endures.*
>
> *(Tom Newton – 1725-1807)*

***

Bud had been found twice: once as a little five-year-old child in these mountain woods by men in the community; and once as a sinner by God his Father who brought him home by the precious blood of His Son, the sacrificial Lamb.

God is sovereign. His earthly assignment for Bud was the spreading of the gospel. Physically, Bud couldn't speak clearly; spiritually he shouted!

Once a great teacher of preachers, gave an assignment. "Go and preach the gospel; but, only use words when necessary." Bud made one hundred percent on the final.

***

The funeral procession to the graveside service was over two miles long, setting the county record! The sun went away and gray clouds moved in as everyone made their way to the graveside, It was as though God was announcing, "My son Bud's smile is no longer with you. He is here, with his ear-to-ear grin sitting around My throne of grace."

Bud's body was laid in the Lone Valley Cemetery. Not many tears were shed, because Bud's chains were gone. He was set free to speak, run, laugh and sing, on pitch, with the angel choir. Best of all he was serving his Father around the throne of grace.

Several members of the Zafra Church donated money for his headstone. The quotes engraved on it read:

> *The best part of beauty is*
> *that which no picture can express.*
> *- Bacon*

CHAPTER FIFTEEN

- POSTLUDE -

Jesus said,
"...He has sent me to heal the broken hearted...
to comfort and console those who mourn,
to give them beauty for ashes, the oil of
joy for mourning, the garment of praise
for the spirit of heaviness..."
~ Isaiah 61:1-3 (NKJV) ~

What a privilege it is for me to have known Bud. I look back on his story with honor and joy. Bud, my friend; illiterate, speech-impaired, alone, poor---I could go on---taught me the unmeasurable sovereignty of God; a fountain flowing deep and wide.

The list below is the top 12 things Bud taught me. There are more, however, these are the ones which have helped me most in my walk with my Shepherd ...through the valley of the shadow of death.

Bud taught me...

#12 ...I should be thankful and always grateful for what God has given to me as my work.

Bud's goats were not a means to an end. His goats were joy, fellowship and comfort. God sustained his livelihood.

#11 ...to sing no matter what.

He sang all the time, not pretty, not on pitch, not words to be understood, but from his heart. Every note beautiful.

#10 ...to realize having no money doesn't mean you're not rich.

Bud never had money, but he had everything he needed.

#9 ...*to never leave anyone out; everyone is important.*

Bud never met a stranger. He would always walk up to a church visitor and shake their hand hard. Miraculously, he never forgot their name.

#8 ...*to remain faithful.*

Bud NEVER missed church. If his ride didn't show, he would walk. He always had faith his Father would provide a way.

#7 ...*life was not about how I looked or smelled.*

He smelled like his goats. It never bothered him that His clothes were mix and match, torn or dirty. Bud never gave his wardrobe a thought. Duty came first! His face had no beauty. Yet as soon as Bud became your friend, his face changed from earthy to radiant.

#6 ...*to know humans and animals by their name.*

Bud never forgot your name. All of Bud's animals had names. It didn't matter if they were goats.

#5 ...*to find happiness in the task ahead.*

Each day when Bud came to feed his goats, bleating began before they could even see him. The bleating "baa" sounded as if they were calling "Buh---uh—duh" their shepherd's name.

#4 ...*to be a servant of the Lord.*

Bud wanted to serve: he taught the children to obey; he opened his Bible even when he couldn't read; he served in any capacity to the best of his ability.

#3 ...*to never retaliate.*

Bud never said--- "...I'll pay you back for this wrong! He waited for the Lord, and He avenged him." (Proverbs 20:22 – NIV paraphrased)

#2 ...*to ALWAYS wear a smile.*

Bud's ear-to-ear grin was of the Spirit. It was as catching as a forest fire out of control!

#1... THE MOST IMPORTANT LIFE LESSON BUD TAUGHT ME:

"...love the Lord my God with all my heart and with all my soul and with all my strength and with all my mind, and to love my neighbor as myself." (Luke 10:27 – NIV paraphrased)

Bud's love never waned. He continued on the straight and narrow path of righteousness. The lyrics to one of his favorite hymns, *Footsteps of Jesus*, conveys Bud's example throughout his life:

Footprints of Jesus that make the pathway glow;
We will follow the steps of Jesus where'er they go

(Mary Slade – 1826-1882/Asa Everett – 1828-1875)

Bud followed his Shepherd, through the valley of the shadow of death to dwell in His house forever.

***

There is a place here in the valley of the shadow of death where roses are gathered in the darkest hours of the night, because if they are gathered in the light of day, they lose most of their fragrance.

As the Shepherd gathered Bud into his arms out of this dark valley of the shadow of death, the sweet-smelling aroma of this beautiful rose's fragrance exploded at his Father's throne of grace. When he stepped from the darkness into the light, he was in full bloom.

Listen as Bud sings:

If you could see me now,
I'm walking streets of gold.
...I'm standing tall and whole.
...You'd know I've seen His face.
...The pain has been erased.
You wouldn't want me to ever leave this perfect place.
If you could see me now.

(Kim Noblitt - 1992)

ABOUT THE AUTHOR

Dr. Cynthia Ann Perkins grew up in the southeastern corner of Oklahoma in the Kiamichi Mountains. There, her family were missionaries in a small community called Zafra. Bud was a part of her family both personally and church. Her beginning education was in Zafra's one-room schoolhouse, the same place where Bud had gone several years earlier.

At the age of eighteen, she left for college, where she met her husband, Kent Perkins. They both embraced the ministry. After marriage, she received her PhD in Music Education from the University of Oklahoma. Cynthia and Kent have been missionaries in both Nicaragua and the Kiamichis. Cynthia has taught music to all ages in public schools, colleges, and churches. She has also been the Christian education minister in the churches where her husband has been called to minister.

Cynthia has been published by Standard Publishing Company and numerous community newspapers and magazines. *STILL WATERS,* her first book, is a 365 daily devotional study over the Twenty-third Psalm. Cynthia is a speaker and singer for any churches, groups or organizations. Contact her at 918-755-4462 or cperkinsphd@yahoo.com.

Kent and Cynthia have two children: Ann Marie Brown, married to Sig, and Keri Lynn Lawson, married to Jake. She has four wonderful grandchildren: Brodie and Audrey Anna Brown and Dewey Wayne and Lucille Lynn Lawson. She and her husband Kent live between Nashoba and Honobia, Oklahoma. They currently minister at the Zafra Church in Zafra, Oklahoma, the church where Bud was a member. The church of her childhood.